ULTIMATE BASS FISHING LIBRARY

GUIDE TO TOPWATER FISHING

CHOOSING AND USING
SURFACE LURES FOR BASS

MONTGOMERY, ALABAMA

INTRODUCTION
Topwater Harmony

THEY SPUTTER, plop, gurgle and churn across the water. Such is the symphony of topwater baits. There is but one force capable of interrupting the easily recognizable music made by these lures as they move across the surface. And that is the sound of an irritated or curious bass slamming the noisy floating object that has invaded its turf.

Some bass strike topwaters out of aggression while others eat the baits because they resemble food. Regardless of the reason, what results is a two-way contest between a leaping fish flexing every muscle in its body and an angler who is experiencing the ultimate bass fishing moment.

Chugger, prop bait, weedless spoon or buzzbait — the category of topwater does not matter. What does is the exhilaration of working a floating lure across the surface and knowing that at any moment a bass will appear from nowhere and crash the bait.

Of all lures, topwaters are undeniably the most fun to fish. They are also among the few lures whose action is totally dependent on the hand movements of the angler. In a way, the mechanics of topwater fishing are not unlike the fluid hand motions made by a musician playing an instrument.

A violin is attentive to every move made by the artist's hands as the notes come forth to make the harmonious music. Should he make a wrong move with the bow, the instrument will play off-key. In bass fishing terms, this is like breaking the cadence of a walking bait just as it enters the strike zone — a sour note to the fish.

This book will help you make perfect music with topwaters. Best of all, it is a sign of things to come in the Ultimate Bass Fishing Library. This book is the first in a series that will take readers through categories of lures such as spinnerbaits, jigs, crankbaits, soft plastics and more.

Decades of information, wisdom and experimentation by the pros are all contained herein. This book is of particular value because topwaters, unlike other hard baits, come in myriad styles. Some come with props while others have appendages protruding from their bodies. Others, like the weedless spoon, are simple slabs of plastic and metal.

If you are a believer that variety is the spice of life, then topwaters are for you. The only challenge to topwater fishing, if there really is one, is how to choose from the numerous options.

This book will point you in the right direction. Then, all you will need to do is tie on the right weapon and make your own music.

Copyright 2004 by BASS

Published in 2004 by BASS
5845 Carmichael Road
Montgomery, AL 36117

Editor In Chief:
Dave Precht

Editor:
James Hall

Managing Editor:
Craig Lamb

Editorial Assistant:
Althea Goodyear

Art Director:
Rick Reed

Designers:
Laurie Willis, Leah Cochrane,
Bill Gantt, Nancy Lavender

Illustrators:
Chris Armstrong, Shannon Barnes,
Lenny McPherson

Photography Manager:
Gerald Crawford

Contributing Writers:
Chris Altman, William C. Blizzard,
Wade Bourne, Paul A. Cañada,
David Hart, Mark Hicks, Bruce Ingram,
Keith Jackson, Michael Jones,
Kenneth L. Kieser, John Neporadny Jr.,
Dave Precht, Steve Price, Mark Rizk,
Bernie Schultz, Louie Stout,
Tim Tucker, Don Wirth

Contributing Photographers:
Chris Altman, Charles Beck,
Wade Bourne, Paul A. Cañada,
Soc Clay, Gerald Crawford, Tom Evans,
James Hall, David Hart, Mark Hicks,
Bruce Ingram, Michael Jones,
Kenneth L. Kieser, Bill Lindner,
Peter B. Mathiesen, John Neporadny Jr.,
Steve Price, David J. Sams, Doug Stamm,
Louie Stout, Gary Tramontina,
Tim Tucker, Don Wirth

Copy Editors:
Laura Harris, Debbie Salter

Manufacturing Manager:
Bill Holmes

Marketing:
Betsy B. Peters

**Vice President &
General Manager, BASS:**
Dean Kessel

Printed on American paper by
RR Donnelley

ISBN 1-890280-05-4

WHY WE LOVE topwater fishing: The dance of a bass above the surface of the water, moved by the rhythm of your bait.

CONTENTS

ALL ABOUT TOPWATERS

Floating lures
are making a comeback . . .

THE TOPWATER RESURGENCE

Surface fishing went out of style
with the tournament crowd.
That was until the topwater renaissance

TOSSING SURFACE PLUGS is one of bass fishing's most thrilling techniques. In fact, it is the very essence of the sport. Yet this staple of angling fell by the wayside as more techniques entered the angling mainstream in the 1980s and 1990s. Deep cranking and finesse fishing were two of the culprits that stole the limelight.

But now the topwater is back. Surface bait aficionados are once again enjoying the thrill of having a bass slurp in a popper or chugger without feeling guilty for not dredging up the bottom. The following insight from the pros proves the point.

PROS' PERSPECTIVES

Most important bass fishing trends begin on the tournament trail, and the recent resurgence in topwater lures is no exception. "BASS pros are now fishing topwater lures a lot more seriously than in the past," claims Alabama pro Gerald Swindle. "Recent developments in the surface bait market have greatly broadened their appeal." Swindle mentions the following:

• *More sizes* — "This factor has had a tremendous impact on the frequency with which I fish a topwater lure. Before, you only had one, maybe two sizes available in most popular surface lures. Now you can get any style — popper, stickbait, prop bait — in virtually any size you want. This enables you to fine-tune topwater lure size to conditions, just as you routinely do with a soft plastic bait or a crankbait. The new, smaller surface baits are especially hot; many of our bass lakes are either highly pressured or clear, and these are especially effective under tough conditions."

• *Longer seasons* — "There was a time when you didn't even think about throwing a surface lure until the water

(Opposite page) TOPWATERS, like other lure categories, have undergone a facelift and come in myriad colors. The plethora of available hues gives anglers more options from which to choose.

Topwater Tips

The first bass tournament organized by BASS founder Ray Scott, the All American at Beaver Lake, Ark., was won with a topwater plug. Tennessee angler Stan Sloan used a Bomber Spin Stick to claim the first prize of $10,000 in June 1967. Since that time, almost all BASS tournaments have been won with subsurface lures. More recently, however, pro anglers have been working surface baits into their repertoires. They've discovered that topwaters often produce bigger bass.

TOPWATERS ARE ideal for float tubing because the season coincides with this summertime, shallow water technique.

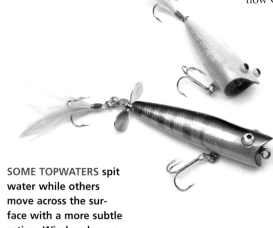

SOME TOPWATERS spit water while others move across the surface with a more subtle action. Wind and wave action dictate which lure style is best.

hit the 60 degree range. But there was a BASS event on Grand Lake, Okla., several years ago that proved to be a watershed event in topwater fishing. The night before the tournament began, a massive cold front blew through. It snowed like crazy, and air temperatures plummeted into the teens during all three days of competition, yet the tournament was won on a buzzbait. You can bet that opened a lot of eyes! I use topwaters a lot earlier now, and I stay with 'em a lot later in the year."

• *Better designs* — "Remember when bass fishermen talked with reverence about how Charlie Campbell could work a Zara Spook? Many topwater lure styles have traditionally required a great deal of angler skill to fish properly, but even a novice can make the newest designs on the market perform great. When a lure is easy to fish, it has a broader appeal."

Swindle favors imported Lucky Craft surface lures. "I've been to their factory in Japan, and I'm convinced Japanese lures are worth every penny of the premium price they command," he indicates. "In Japan, lure design is not a matter of gimmickry or marketing hype — it's an art. Their designers are highly dedicated to their craft. Designing a lure that

provokes a positive response from bass is serious business to them. Bass fishing is huge in Japan, and their waters receive unbelievable fishing pressure. It takes lures with finely crafted subtleties in appearance and action to make their bass bite. If a surface lure works there, you can darn sure bet it'll work here."

One of Swindle's favorite topwaters is Lucky Craft's 1 1/2-inch Bevy Pop, a miniature popper. "Take a reservoir like Douglas Lake, Tenn., where bass school on small shad minnows," he says. "You can cast a 2- or 3-inch popper until your arm falls off and not get a bite, but bass will jump all over the miniature Bevy Pop. It's only recently that we've had access to smaller, finesse-type surface lures like this one. They've made a major impact in reviving the surface lure market."

Swindle also favors Lucky Craft's Sammy 65, a 2 1/2-inch walking bait. "Its finish is deep and translucent, much like a live shad. Domestic lure makers are producing topwaters with nice finishes, but they have a long way to go before they match the exquisite finishes of Japanese lures," he notes.

"The spread of zebra mussels has aided the resurgence of topwater fishing on the pro bass circuit," claims Kentucky pro Mark Menendez. "These mollusks filter sediment from the water, making it very clear, and clear water is definitely surface bait water. Topwater lures are awesome search baits — you can pull in fish from a greater distance on a surface bait than with other lure styles. Bass often suspend in clear lakes, and will swim incredible distances to smash a topwater lure."

The fact that surface baits have a reputation for catching lunker bass hasn't gone unnoticed by BASS pros, Menendez adds. "The surface is a real easy place for a big, lazy bass to grab a meal. I once caught an 8-pounder on a Zara Spook during practice for a BASS event on Old Hickory Lake, Tenn. I know several fishermen who have caught 10-pounders on Pop-Rs. If you're gunning for a monster bass in today's highly pressured climate, a surface lure would be a great bet."

Menendez begins fishing a topwater lure once the water temp nudges the 50 degree mark in spring. "The word hasn't really gotten out yet to weekend fishermen about how good topwater fishing can be in early spring," he says. "You can catch some real wall-hangers on surface baits in prespawn, but you *must* slow your presentation way down. In 50 degree water, I'll fish a buzzbait so the blades barely move."

Most fishermen view ideal surface lure conditions as glassy-smooth, but you'll often experience a more active topwater bite in choppy water, Menendez adds. "Use the noisiest lures in your tacklebox — big, aggressive prop baits like the Devil's Horse are dynamite in rough water. I've caught bass on buzzbaits in a foot-high chop."

SOMETIMES BUZZBAITS need to be burned across the surface. Other times they need to be retrieved very slowly, blades barely turning. Let the bass tell you which presentation they want.

The Kentucky pro believes the water can get too hot for a reliable surface bite. "When the lake temp rises above 85 degrees, I don't mess with topwaters much," he says. "In extreme temperatures, bass begin shutting down their metabolism to avoid stress. Their strike zone shrinks dramatically, and they refuse to chase down prey. My best topwater bite typically occurs between 58 and 72 degrees in both spring and fall."

Something about surface lures inspires creativity in bass anglers, Menendez says. "Zell Rowland was one of the first guys on the pro tour to modify his topwater plugs, carving the lip out of a Pop-R so it would spit water. I won my first major tournament on a weird rig involving a Zara Spook; I was only 21 at the time, and I entered as a nonboater. I ran a 15-inch leader off the back hook of a Spook and tied a Jack Chancellor Do-Nothing worm to the leader with a split shot in front of it. On my first cast, I hung a good bass on the Spook. My partner reached for the net, and I said, 'Hang on, I'm not finished yet!' Suddenly a second bass took the worm, and I landed 'em both. For 10 casts in a row I caught at least one bass, sometimes two, on that silly rig, and I won the tournament. I've been a believer in surface lures ever since."

VISUAL FINESSE BAITS

"Topwater lures are the finesse baits of the New Millennium," claims Cliff Soward, product manager for PRADCO, one of the world's largest lure manufacturers. "Unlike a bottom-bumping bait, you can see exactly what your topwater lure is doing, and you can immediately visualize every change, no matter how minor, that takes place in its action when you alter the retrieve."

Knowledgeable bass anglers are learning that size matters when it comes to surface lures, Soward says. "There's a huge trend toward smaller surface lures among skilled bassers, driven in part by the press about those pricey Japanese plugs. Small surface baits work great because the average size of our bass is smaller than it once was."

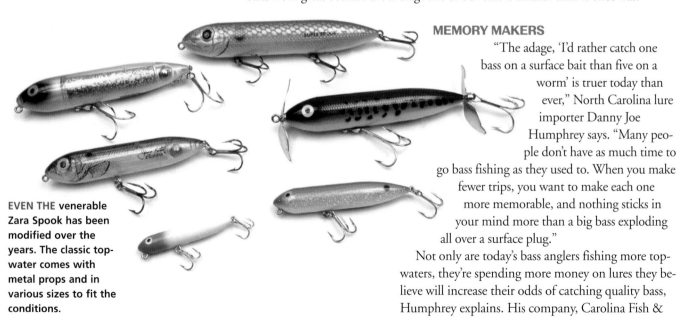

EVEN THE venerable Zara Spook has been modified over the years. The classic topwater comes with metal props and in various sizes to fit the conditions.

MEMORY MAKERS

"The adage, 'I'd rather catch one bass on a surface bait than five on a worm' is truer today than ever," North Carolina lure importer Danny Joe Humphrey says. "Many people don't have as much time to go bass fishing as they used to. When you make fewer trips, you want to make each one more memorable, and nothing sticks in your mind more than a big bass exploding all over a surface plug."

Not only are today's bass anglers fishing more topwaters, they're spending more money on lures they believe will increase their odds of catching quality bass, Humphrey explains. His company, Carolina Fish &

Fur, imports exotic Viva lures; some Viva surface baits cost as much as $25 apiece. "The detailing on these lures is remarkable," Humphrey says. "They've got little design nuances that really make a difference on pressured bass. For example, the Viva Bug I rests in the water at a 15 degree angle, while other poppers sit at about a 60 degree slant. This makes the Bug I much quicker to react when you move the rod tip. It also has a feather tail that throws a shadow, resembling a live baitfish; this breathes even when the lure is sitting still."

Many anglers may not be aware of the subtle variations now available in surface lures, Humphrey says. "You might think all poppers are created equal, but a Pop-R makes considerably more noise than a Bug I, which makes more splash than pop. Therefore, these two lures cover two entirely different bass fishing scenarios: The Pop-R mimics another predator, such as a small bass striking prey on the surface; while the Bug I creates the impression of a frightened baitfish. Bass will absolutely plaster a Pop-R, while they suck in a Bug I like a fly fishing popping bug. Serious anglers know that bass feeding on top are often highly selective. Just as you wouldn't fish a tournament without a full range of soft plastic lures or crankbaits, having a variety of topwaters in your arsenal allows you to fine-tune your presentation, and it definitely gives you an edge on your competition."

Speaking of competition, Humphrey also runs a regional tournament circuit with 350 regular contenders, and has seen a major shift toward topwater fishing in these events.

"We have a five bass limit here in North Carolina, and tournament fishermen know that 10 pounds usually isn't going to put them in the money," he says. "Where they used to say, 'I'm gonna catch my limit and then spend the rest of the day trying to catch a big bass,' they're *now* going after big bass *first* by banking on the early morning topwater bite. Then, once the sun gets overhead, they fill out their limit by catching keepers on bottom-bumping stuff. So I guess you could say topwater baits have turned tournament fishing upside-down."

Candid Comments About Topwaters

Surface plugs are a foundation of the successful tournament résumé of Kentucky pro Mark Menendez. Read on for his take on the various topwater baits comprising his favorite lure category.

■ On buzzbaits — "Bass will turn off a buzzbait quicker than any other topwater lure. I don't use 'em unless I know I'm in an area that might hold a big bass. I get too excited fishing buzzbaits; when a bass hits, I have a tendency to jerk the buzzer out of its mouth."

■ On spitting baits — "Remember when guys in California were selling 'em out of the trunks of their cars at launch ramps for $50 apiece? Now you can get a good spitter for $6. You have to be careful with spitters, though. They often provoke a real aggressive bite the first day of a tournament, but fish lose interest in them quickly, once they get pressured."

■ On surface bait size — "What goes around, comes around. Now that the smaller topwaters have caught on, the bass in many lakes are getting used to them, and I'm having to go back to the bigger surface lures to catch bigger bass."

■ On floating minnows — "With the emphasis on suspending jerkbaits, these have been almost totally forgotten, but man, are they ever deadly. On a trip to Lake Seminole (Ga.), I once took a big floating Rogue, cast it out on stump flats, gave it a hard jerk and let it float back up, nice and easy. I caught a bunch of 6- and 7-pounders on this pattern."

■ On bedding bass — "Another great scenario for a floating minnow. To warm 'em up, I'll get 'em agitated by twitching the Rogue on top, then switch to a lizard or finesse worm to seal the deal."

■ On smallmouth — "A Zara Spook is so deadly on big smallmouth, it'll scare you. Blue shore minnow, that's my smallmouth color."

■ On overhanging cover — "A lot of guys skip a floating worm under tree branches in spring; I like a Pop-R. I use a roll cast to get it way back in there."

■ On time of day — "Bass fishermen are conditioned to fishing topwaters early and late in the day. I've fished tournaments with guys who have actually quit using a surface bait that they were actively catching fish on, just because the sun rose over the treeline! I'll fish 'em as long as the bass want 'em, which is often all day long. On many northern lakes, the best topwater bite often occurs in midday, under bright blue skies."

■ On Jitterbugs — "Guys who think they're hotshot bass fishermen sometimes joke about the ultimate loser bass pattern: trolling Jitterbugs by the dam. Well, I've got a half-dozen Jitterbugs in my tacklebox right now. It's one of my favorites on stormy days."

SWINGING FOR THE FENCE WITH TOPWATERS

When they need a big bass to anchor their limits, some top pros turn to surface baits

HOMER HUMPHREYS REMEMBERS the day well. The wind was howling across North Carolina's Lake Norman, but the bass were still biting — at least they were still biting Humphreys' lure, a new topwater plug known locally as "The Bird," but since renamed the "Sputter Ace." His catch that day averaged 2 1/2

pounds per bass, unusually heavy for Lake Norman.

Mark Davis' best outing with a topwater lure included a 9-pounder that smashed a Boy Howdy; and in one September day to remember, Jim Morton and a friend boated more than 50 bass on a weighted Chug Bug — and the fish were still hitting when they left.

No matter how many tournaments are won on jigs, crankbaits or soft plastics, every serious tournament pro still keeps a supply of sputtering, popping, chugging surface lures nearby.

"There is the obvious thrill of seeing a bass hit a lure," explains California pro Rich Tauber, "but in competition, the real reasons we use topwater lures are because some of them, such as the Zara Spook, are big bass baits. Also, topwater lures will attract bass from longer distances than will most other lures.

"At Lake Mead, for example, you can actually see bass come up from 20 to 30 feet to hit a topwater plug. I don't know of any other category of lure that will do that."

The pros classify topwater lures into several categories, such as "chuggers" (Rebel Pop-R, Storm Chug Bug, Heddon Chugger), "splashers" (Rico), "prop baits," (Smithwick Devil's Horse, Woodchopper, Heddon Tiny Torpedo) and "minnow imitations" (Rapala, Storm ThunderStick, Bomber Long A). Because each lure performs a particular way, they are actually quite specialized and generally used only under certain conditions.

"Most successful topwater anglers agree the real key to using any surface lure — other than a buzzbait — is developing a rhythm or cadence when working the lure, coordinating both your rod tip movement and your reel so the lure 'works' for you," says Tauber.

"In reality, it's not the rhythm of the lure that is so important, but rather the rhythm of the angler. It forces him to concentrate harder on working the lure, and the more you concentrate the more fish you'll catch. Except for jigs, most lures don't force you to concentrate that hard.

"All topwater lures, with the exception of buzzbaits, work best when fished on a slack line," continues Tauber, "but there is no limit to the number of ways you can work a topwater lure. That's what makes them both difficult and exciting to use."

With these thoughts in mind, here's how several top pros fish their favorite surface lures:

JIM MORTON: WEIGHTED CHUG BUG

"I like to fish the Chug Bug under oddball conditions, such as in calm water under a bright sky, primarily because I know few other fishermen will be doing the same thing. My favorite seasons are summer and fall, but I'll really fish the lure anytime I see bass actively chasing baitfish.

"I believe one of the keys to successful topwater fishing with lures like the Chug Bug is the presence of baitfish. In the summer and fall, bass are chasing shad, and I don't think the fish are really looking at the shad so much as they're hearing them, so you

Topwater Tips

Rapala/Storm fishing pro Jim Morton often adds weight to the tail end of his Storm Chug Bugs to make them work differently. He affixes one or more Storm SuspenDots on the belly of the plug, near the tail hook, to make the bait ride tail-down in the water. This enables him to work the lure with more action — and without moving the plug very far with each twitch. The same trick can be applied to other topwaters, including twitch baits, stickbaits and poppers, to give fish a different "look" than they're accustomed to seeing. What's more, bass seem to become hooked more easily, since the bait's tail rides lower in the water.

Pick A Color

Many anglers believe that bass strike a topwater because of its noise or action, and that lure color makes little difference. Most pros would disagree. Here are some guidelines from topwater guru Zell Rowland for using the right color at the right time:

■ **Clear water, sunny day** — Use realistic finishes with plenty of flash (silver, gold, blue).

■ **Clear water, cloudy day** — Avoid reflective colors and use flat finishes (bone white, black).
■ **Clear water, smallmouth bass** — Smallmouth love "hot" colors, especially bright yellow and chartreuse.
■ **Murky water** — Give the bass plenty of opportunity to find the lure by using a dark color (black, purple) which shows up better in low visibility conditions.
■ **"Following" bass** — Bass often follow a topwater lure without striking it, especially in clear lakes. A color change can provoke a strike. If the lure the bass followed is black or bone white, switch to a reflective finish like chrome, or vice versa.

can make a long cast and work the lure back fast.

"Although I look for baitfish, practically any type of fish activity tells me a topwater lure will work. In the spring, just the opposite is true. Bass are more cover-oriented then, so you have to work the lure slower.

"Even when there is no visible fish activity, you can fish topwater lures around flat, rocky points, concentrating on potential ambush sites along the edges or near heavy cover. Bass won't always have shad trapped in the back of a cove or pocket.

"Early in the morning, I start 'walking' a Chug Bug back as soon as it hits the water, and I walk it all the way to the boat. The brighter the sun becomes, the faster my retrieve. I use a 6-foot, 6-inch medium/heavy action Abu Garcia graphite rod with a fast tip. You have to develop the

JIM MORTON fishes a weighted Chug Bug when other anglers opt for other lures. Clear, slick water conditions are optimum for this approach.

patience to wait an extra instant before setting the hook on a strike. Using a rod like this, it's easy to take the lure away from the fish.

"I prefer 15- or 16-pound-test line, tying directly to the lure to have better control, and I work the Chug Bug with quick wrist movements with the rod held down."

MARK DAVIS: BOY HOWDY

"The most important thing to do with a Boy Howdy is balance the lure so that when it's resting in the water, it sits nearly at a 90 degree angle, with only about an inch of the nose out of the water. Originally,

THE EXPERTS agree that coordinating rod tip movement with speed of retrieve is the real key to using any surface lure.

HOMER HUMPHREYS is a fan of the Sputter Ace because it combines the features of a topwater, spinnerbait and buzzbait.

the lure was made weighted, and these are still available in some stores, but if you can't find one, adding a 1/8-ounce bullet worm sinker usually works fine.

"Just remove the rear treble, slip the weight onto the wire harness and replace the hook. To improve the hooking power of the lure, I usually change the standard No. 6 hooks with No. 4 hooks, and I leave the front treble off entirely.

"Basically, this is a cast-and-twitch lure, but it's very erratic. It's not a walking action, but rather, a bobbing, darting movement: Each time you twitch the lure, it has to first come out of the water, then dart to one side or the other.

"I use a 6-foot, medium action Falcon graphite pistol grip rod, and once I start moving the bait, I don't stop. If a bass boils and misses, I may slow my retrieve, but I rarely stop it completely.

"For me, the best time to use a Boy Howdy is the month following the spawn, but I also like it in the summer when bass are schooling, and

Busting The Top

Topwater lures really shine when bass are schooling in numbers on top, gorging on baitfish. Here are some tips from veteran Texas pro Zell Rowland:

"Be careful when approaching schooling bass, especially in clear lakes. Don't run right up on the school with your big motor and expect the fish to stay on the surface. Instead, maneuver within casting range with your electric trolling motor. Make sure your reel is properly adjusted so you don't backlash — this often happens when an angler gets excited and tries to cast too far to surfacing fish.

"A long, medium/light action baitcasting rod with plenty of give to the tip permits extra-long casts; combine this with a baitcasting reel spooled with fairly light line for maximum distance. This soft-action rod will also help you land fish that are only lightly hooked, a common occurrence in 'jump fishing.'

"Some topwater styles, especially poppers and stickbaits, are heavier than others and can be cast farther. Try to anticipate the direction in which the school is moving and lead the fish slightly. And if schooling fish refuse to strike your topwater presentation, immediately switch to a sinking lure, such as a lipless crankbait or grub."

HEAVY TOPWATERS like the Pop-R can be cast greater distances, a real asset when targeting schooling bass.

Topwater Targets

Topwaters can be fished in a surprisingly large number of bass fishing scenarios, including the following:

■ **Close to shoreline cover** — Fish topwaters around stumps, laydown logs, submerged brushpiles and other shallow cover.

■ **Over surface weeds** — Weedless topwaters can be skimmed across thick surface vegetation without hanging up.

■ **Over submerged vegetation** — Bass often hide in open pockets in thick beds of hydrilla and milfoil and may rise up to smash a topwater bait.

■ **Over offshore structures** — Topwater baits are often effective in areas where a crankbait or worm might be used — on long points, over humps and ledges, etc.

■ **Offshore, for suspending or schooling bass** — When bass chase large schools of baitfish into open water, they'll often strike a topwater lure.

again in September and October when bass are really chasing shad.

"This is not really a good shallow water lure, like the Pop-R; I seldom have much success in water less than 5 feet deep. I classify the Boy Howdy as an open water lure for clear water, but you can also fish it around grasslines and boat docks where bass may be hiding and waiting for shad.

"I prefer 14-pound-test line, and I tie straight to the lure. You twitch it with your rod tip down and on a slack line, which is what gives the lure its erratic movement."

HOMER HUMPHREYS: SPUTTER ACE

"This lure is really a combination of topwater plug, spinnerbait and buzzbait. That's because it floats, and it has a front-mounted buzzbait blade and a spinnerbait skirt covering the rear treble. It's better than a buzzbait, however, because you can use a stop-and-go retrieve, and each time you do stop it, the rear skirt breathes and opens up.

"The way I like to fish a Sputter Ace is by making a long cast, then immediately raising my rod and pulling the lure about 2 feet across the surface. To me, this really gets the attention of a bass. Then, I walk the lure with little twitches the same way you walk a Spook. The in-line propeller sounds just like a shad flicking across the water.

"On bright days, bass tend to follow this lure, and when they do, I usually stop the retrieve, then suddenly drag the lure quickly across the surface, trying to imitate something escaping. That's when they nail it.

"There are dozens of ways to fish the lure, because it works in water down to 57 or 58 degrees, and it's effective in both shallow and deep water. I really like to fish it on shallow, brushy flats because it comes through these places just like a buzzbait, but it doesn't sound like one. And there isn't a better topwater lure made for fishing rough, choppy water."

Topwater Lessons On The Big O

Florida's giant Lake Okeechobee is a topwater fisherman's paradise. You can chunk plugs at bragging-size bass all day, and all year when conditions are right.

Conditions were far from perfect one spring day when local expert Glenn Hunter set out to teach his companion a few lessons about topwater fishing. A classic spring cold front had roared through the day before, leaving in its wake clear-blue, mile-high skies, frigid north winds and rising barometric pressure. The kiss of death in Florida for any type of fishing.

"This may be one long, tough day of topwater fishing," said Glen Hunter to his partner as they idled away from the boat ramp. "But I know some shallow, sheltered spots back in some bulrush islands that have been holding some bass. Whether the fish are still there in this cold weather I don't know, but they're good places to check first.

"The water temperature there should be a little warmer than out on the main lake, so maybe the bass will be a bit more active and will hit a topwater lure better than elsewhere."

He tied a small, clear, Heddon Tiny Torpedo plug onto 8-pound-test line and fired a long cast toward his target. That cast brought an aggressive strike from a 4-pounder. Over the next few hours, the pair boated a half-dozen bass, and lost several others, including another good fish of about 4 pounds.

Through persistence on a day when even the fishermen with flipping sticks weren't getting many strikes, Hunter provided valuable, on-the-water lessons in surface fishing. Following are a few.

■ Be alert — Many fish caught that day hit small, lightweight plugs aimed at places the anglers had seen fish striking, or simply moving in shallow water.

■ Concentrate on the shallows — In any weather, shallow bass are generally more active than those in deeper water. Few lures outdo topwaters in attracting aggressive strikes from hungry bass.

■ Search for shade — It's no secret that topwater fishing is more productive at dawn and dusk, when the sun is low on the horizon. But you can find ideal conditions for fooling bass by working a topwater plug into and through shady areas adjacent to timber, docks, bridge pilings and the like.

■ Work with the wind — By disrupting the surface with waves and ripples, a moderate wind can em-

bolden bass enough to hit topwaters at any time of day. Look for windblown areas along riprap, bluff banks, long points and weed edges, where bass and baitfish will congregate.

■ Keep on the move — Bass in deep water tend to gather in bunches, but feeding fish disperse throughout the shallows. The more pieces of cover you can brush with a surface plug, the more fish you'll catch.

■ Make long, accurate casts — Shallow bass are spooky, especially in clear water. If you can't make long casts with baitcasting gear, switch to long spinning rods with lighter line.

■ Sharp hooks are imperative — When a bass hits at the end of a long cast, you have to move a lot of line to get the hook into the fish's mouth. A long rod helps, but supersharp hooks make the chore much easier.

■ Don't set the hook too soon — One reason many people miss surface strikes is that they haul back on the rod as soon as they see the splash. Bass often miss in their first attempt at a surface plug, and a premature hook set will merely pull the bait away from the fish. Force yourself to wait until you're sure the bass has the bait before setting the hook.

■ See fish before they see you — Good polarized sunglasses can enable you to spot fish (or at least, their hideouts) before they can see you. Train yourself to pick out the profiles of bass in shallow water.

■ Don't rule out surface fishing — As Hunter proved emphatically, topwater plugging can pay off in even the worst of conditions, especially on the Big O.

WINDBLOWN AREAS along weedlines are ideal topwater targets on large impoundments like Lake Okeechobee.

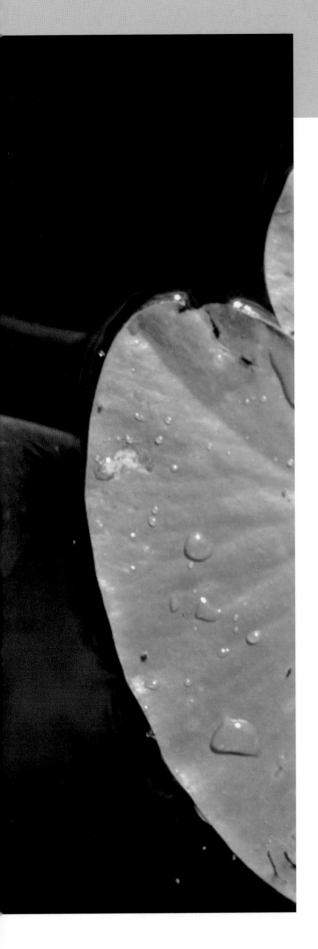

PICKING THE RIGHT BAIT

How to match the hatch
with the right bait . . .

NOT ALL TOPWATER baits work all the time. But the bass don't know that.

CHOOSING AND USING TOPWATER LURES

While many lures will work when the topwater bite is on, experts know how to choose precisely the right style of surface bait

GETTING BASS FISHERMEN TO AGREE ON ANYTHING is often a difficult proposition. Unless of course, you're talking about topwater fishing and the excitement that a water-churning strike can generate. At least in this one regard, anglers speak with a unified voice: They like it. A lot.

Of course, who could argue? The art of topwater fishing is the one angling discipline in which the entire fish catching process — from strike to net — has a witness. With both eyes wide open, a bass fisherman gets to see it all from start to finish.

(Opposite page) WATER CLARITY generally needs to be in the clear to slightly stained category for optimum success with topwaters.

But the allure of the surface strike goes beyond just the visual component. There is something within every angling soul that takes great satisfaction in simply drawing a fish up to the bait. Not just up, but through that thin barrier between two different worlds.

For a moment, the bass has crashed our party. If the adrenaline doesn't take hold too fast and the mind can overrule the muscle, a solid hook set can mean game-on. It also means that a fisherman knows precisely what's at stake, win or lose. Yes, topwater action is a beautiful thing.

THE ZARA SPOOK is known for bringing fish up from deep water, making it a good choice for deep, clear lakes.

Unfortunately, the lyrical qualities of topwater fishing affect all anglers, including those who manufacture the tackle. For years, the result of this love affair has been a dizzying assortment of topwater baits from the most garish abominations to the most sublime works of art.

Somehow topwater brings out both the very worst and the very best in bait configurations, i.e. the "me-too" school of lure design. Even in antique lure catalogs, topwater plugs dominated the scene with every possible combination of flappers, gizmos and whiz-bang appendages, the result of one manufacturer apparently trying to outdo the next by adding more and bigger of the same.

TWITCHING A topwater minnow will coax strikes when fish are at close range to the lure.

While the marketplace has become somewhat less tolerant of junk lures designed to catch fishermen, there exists an inescapable paradox: At one time or another, no matter how silly the lure, every one of them will catch a bass.

For the serious bass fisherman, however, one's topwater sophistication must be raised to a higher level. It must be elevated above casual use; it should not be limited to early or late summer, to breaking fish or to any of the pigeonholes where anglers file away surface baits. Instead, topwater fishing has to be as much a tactical approach as any other — one where you understand its strengths and weaknesses, yet do not rule out other possibilities.

Of course, this is much easier said than done, because there seems to be a lengthy list of what will work when it comes to topwater tactics. For instance, a veteran topwater fisherman knows that with the right conditions, depending on the time of year, topwater can be the prevailing pattern. And it's occasionally a pattern that can be a day-long affair.

Upon hearing that statement, many bass fishermen would assume that we're talking about cloudy conditions. While that may be true in many instances, anyone who automatically rules out surface baits under bright, clear skies will most certainly overlook a very productive pattern.

So which is it? A stickbait or a minnow bait? Or what about a chugger or buzzbait? Read on. The bases are all covered ahead.

STICKBAIT

One seasonal situation that lends itself to this blue sky surface activity occurs in the postspawn, when bass have exited the primary spawning areas and congregated on key structure nearby. Under these circumstances — or whenever the goal is to call fish to the bait — lure choices should focus on "attack"-style baits, such as the Heddon Zara Spook.

With their sashaying side-to-side action, Spooks have a reputation for producing violent responses from bass. Rather than wanting to eat this lure, many fish apparently look to destroy it, striking with a fury as ferocious as it is determined. Not only do they want to kill the intruder, they will come an appreciable distance to do so.

MINNOW BAIT

More target-oriented in approach is a lure like the Rapala minnow, which can be twitched gently on the surface, coaxing a fish to strike rather than challenging it. Depending on the season

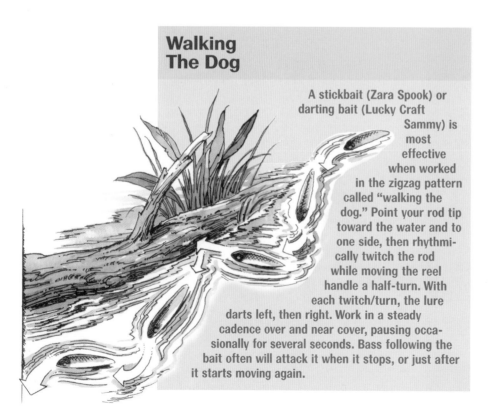

Walking The Dog

A stickbait (Zara Spook) or darting bait (Lucky Craft Sammy) is most effective when worked in the zigzag pattern called "walking the dog." Point your rod tip toward the water and to one side, then rhythmically twitch the rod while moving the reel handle a half-turn. With each twitch/turn, the lure darts left, then right. Work in a steady cadence over and near cover, pausing occasionally for several seconds. Bass following the bait often will attack it when it stops, or just after it starts moving again.

and prevailing weather patterns, bass may not be willing to move far for a meal, or they may exhibit a neutral mood that simply requires time to elicit a response. Of course, it should be noted that the very same, nonaggressive bass could respond very positively to a fast moving buzzbait or walking lure sashaying quickly through the key zone. Another paradox.

Aware of these changing moods, the angler knows his objective is to match the lure type to the conditions and the prevailing mood of the fish themselves. Assuming that a fisherman has considered the prevailing seasonal patterns and placed himself in an area that holds fish, one of the most important elements in selecting any surface lure is water clarity.

Since any surface application is a sight-oriented affair, water clarity generally needs to be in the clear to slightly stained category. As the clarity moves to either extreme of that scale, an angler needs to make decisions on the type of lure selected.

In very clear water, for instance, a bass will often move great distances to a lure, hence a flashy finish and fish-calling action are paramount. However, too much flash and too much commotion in this clear environment may overwhelm bass and deter strikes — especially in very calm, shallow situations.

If conditions require a slower, more deliberate presentation (perhaps bass are holding in shade pockets under bright sun), clear water demands that the lure offer a very natural look — one that can stand up to the scrutiny of the bass.

BUZZBAIT

As water becomes more stained, bass need some help in locating and tracking a topwater lure. The disturbance produced by buzzbaits or prop baits can provide this added dimension. But with more stain to the water there is a greater likelihood of missed strikes — one reason buzzbait fishermen use stinger hooks whenever possible.

Another controlling factor in topwater lure selection is the type and thickness of the cover being fished. Ask any professional about cover,

Windy On Top

The presence of wind and the strength of that wind is yet another element in any topwater scenario. In most cases, a gentle breeze only improves the action by creating just enough surface disturbances to mask any defects in presentation or lure choice. Instead of giving the bass a clear look at the bait, they see only a moving silhouette and the surface disturbance created by the lure movement.

Wind also provides a number of other positive benefits, specifically a cover element for bass that makes them feel more secure in their environment and consequently more willing to chase down lures. There is also an energizing effect to wind, one that stimulates, and in some cases, directs baitfish movement.

As the force of the wind increases, sizing up in lure weight and size may be necessary, not only for casting efficiency, but lure performance as well. Fortunately, the same masking effect that activates the bite and camouflages the exact profile of the lure enables — and often demands — the use of larger baits.

Obviously, the key is recognizing when these changes occur and being able to capitalize on them. Increasing wind, changing cloud conditions — or both — can be vital triggering mechanisms, ones that can quickly turn a poor or mediocre topwater bite into something memorable. And all within a very short period of time.

Minnow Magic

Minnow baits — often called twitch baits because they are designed to be twitched on the surface — closely resemble jerkbaits, which are worked 2 feet deep or more. Most twitch baits are made of buoyant balsa (Rapalas), but plastic models (Red Fins) work well, too. Jerkbaits often are weighted to suspend below the surface, and some sport long diving bills. Fish a minnow bait by moving the rod tip slightly to make the lure dive just underwater. Let it rise to the surface, pause a few seconds, then twitch it again.

Color Matters

Although lure color often becomes an important consideration to many anglers, it is actually one of the least critical. Unless the surface bait in question is a minnow-type bait that can be jerked down under the water, the top or back color of any topwater lure is nearly inconsequential. Even the side colors of a bait only play a small role with walking baits whose side-to-side motion rolls the lure enough to expose these patterns.

In an overwhelming percentage of topwater situations, the only color visible to bass is the bottom or belly color. In nature, virtually every fish that swims — as well as many warmblooded species — has a light-colored underside. As a result, white, pearl-silver or some variation on that theme is often the only vital consideration in selecting topwater lure colors.

Of course, there are certain patterns, such as frog, baby bass, black and clear, that have some important applications and cannot be ignored. For instance, black is an excellent low light or stained water color that provides an identifiable silhouette moving across the water. And clear is a sometimes overlooked choice, particularly in overcast, clear water conditions where flat lighting creates a very realistic, moving illusion.

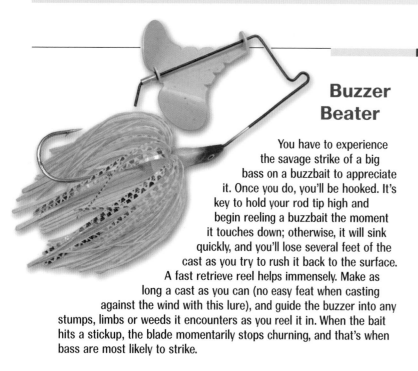

WHEN A bass is hooked on a topwater bait, it will often dance all the way to the boat.

and every one of them will rate grass as the No. 1 target zone. With countless possibilities and any number of cover and depth combinations, finding fish in grass is generally linked to seasonal patterns, sky conditions and the presence of bait.

CHUGGER AND PROP BAIT

In overcast conditions, the bass may roam more extensively, requiring a search-type lure (such as a buzzbait or walking bait) to cover water more thoroughly. If the grass reaches the surface or offers less defined edges, the hunt becomes more target-oriented with holes in the cover or pronounced irregularities in the grassline offering the best opportunities for slower moving lures, such as chuggers, prop baits or minnows.

With a combination of cover types — grass, wood or even rocky structure — lure selection can get more complicated. At times, however, the situation itself may narrow the choices to those baits that can be presented effectively. No matter how difficult the choice may seem, the guiding principles are the same: water clarity, cover, position of the fish on that cover and their willingness (or lack thereof) to move to the bait.

Buzzer Beater

You have to experience the savage strike of a big bass on a buzzbait to appreciate it. Once you do, you'll be hooked. It's key to hold your rod tip high and begin reeling a buzzbait the moment it touches down; otherwise, it will sink quickly, and you'll lose several feet of the cast as you try to rush it back to the surface. A fast retrieve reel helps immensely. Make as long a cast as you can (no easy feat when casting against the wind with this lure), and guide the buzzer into any stumps, limbs or weeds it encounters as you reel it in. When the bait hits a stickup, the blade momentarily stops churning, and that's when bass are most likely to strike.

Choose A Size

Since nearly every topwater lure is offered in different sizes, there is yet another choice to be made. While some anglers adhere to the concept of "matching the hatch" (matching lure size to baitfish size), others function under the credo of "bigger baits, bigger bass." In truth, the conventional wisdom falls somewhere in between.

Perhaps the most obvious example of matching the hatch occurs in the fall season, when schooling bass focus almost exclusively on shad. While any bait thrown into a surface feeding frenzy is likely to get slammed, it is generally more prudent to roughly approximate the size of the forage. This same thinking would apply in certain summer situations in which schooling bass may be selective in their feeding choices.

On the flip side of this equation, those who consistently throw big baits do so with the knowledge that they are pursuing a different kind of fish. It's an "attack" mentality on both ends of the fishing line, with aggressive anglers after fewer but quality bites, and equally aggressive bass willing to make the most of a feeding opportunity. Clearly, this percentage game doesn't always pay off, but when it does, the results are often dramatic.

The yin to this yang often occurs in the spring, when bass can exhibit a full range of moods from highly aggressive to very passive. At times, this finicky situation forces anglers to scale down their offerings, slow down their presentations and quite literally force-feed unwilling fish. By the same token, a large bait can trigger territorial instincts in giant bass at a time when they are most vulnerable.

While it may be an oversimplification, selecting topwater baits doesn't have to be a case of "run it up the flag pole and see who salutes."

With some rather basic information, the choices can be narrowed to a manageable few. From there, the refinement process is guided by the cover, the conditions and the fish themselves. Obviously, an angler needs to make some educated guesses at the very start. But even the guy flying the flag can wet his finger to see which way the wind is blowing.

WALKING BAITS can be tiring to use — but they are well worth the effort.

Proper Plugs

Propeller plugs, like this Tiny Torpedo, churn the water each time you pull them, reminding bass of baitfish skipping across the surface. They're great for schooling bass and a slew of other situations. They're superb fish catchers when you can drop them daintily by a lily pad or other piece of cover, let them rest a few moments, then twitch them slightly. When bass are scattered, however, work them in long, fast twitches back to the boat. Baits with propellers fore and aft, like the Smithwick Devil's Horse, are even better for this pull/pause technique.

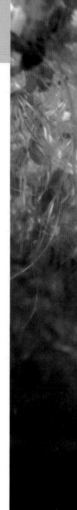

MATCHING TOPWATERS TO CONDITIONS

With a multitude of sizes, colors and attributes, topwaters can be effective most anytime

FEW THINGS STIR a bass fisherman's heart more than topwater fishing. Unfortunately, emotion doesn't put fish in the boat. Logic does. And rest assured, even something as passionate as topwater fishing has a cold, emotionless side to it.

For Zell Rowland and Rich Tauber, two professionals who understand the "business" of topwater, the excitement of a surface strike is always preceded by some careful planning. Most importantly, matching the bait to the conditions.

OVERCOMING MISCONCEPTIONS

• *Early and late* — In some instances, surface action is limited to brief, low light periods in the morning or evening. But, midday topwater bites (even with bright sunshine and clear skies) often produce for anglers who don't limit themselves to the early/late mind-set.

• *Time of year* — Topwater fishing can be productive much earlier and much later in the year. Although water temperatures may affect the overall aggressiveness of bass, they are not absolutes in dictating surface action.

KEY FACTORS

• *Water clarity* — More than anything else, water clarity is the controlling element in topwater fishing. While rattles, props and other noise-producing attributes alert fish and stimulate their curiosity, it is ultimately sight that sells the surface plug to a bass.

Topwater Tips

The Bomber Long A and similar minnow baits can do double duty as a surface and a subsurface lure. In warm water, twitch it to make it dive, then let it float back to the surface. When bass are scattered, you can reel it slowly back, just under the surface. And when water temperatures are cool and bass are lethargic, you can jerk and twitch it beneath the surface, making it dance and pause close to cover.

In more off-colored water, noisy surface plugs, such as buzzbaits, Lucky 13s or Hula Poppers, can be effective, but must be fished closer to targets. These targets don't have to be isolated, just more related to brush and wood as opposed to grass. Since a fish generally has to move farther in grass to strike a lure, good water clarity is required. As a rule, the dirtier the water, the louder the bait required.

• *Water temperature* — "I don't like to use water temperature as a guideline too much, because it changes so much across the country," observes Tauber. "As a general rule, there is a 10 degree difference between the northern part of the country and the southern part. In California, widespread topwater opportunities usually begin

at 65 degrees. But, in the northern regions, it would drop to 55 degrees."

For Rowland, each type of lake is fished similarly, but his tactics always hinge on water temperature. In cooler temperatures (58 to 64 degrees), he opts for something like a jerkbait (Bomber Long A, Rebel Floating Minnow or Smithwick Rogue) that delivers maximum action with minimum movement. As the water temperatures increase, the shift is to larger, faster moving, more aggressive topwater lures, such as Zara Spooks.

• *Lure types* — There are two basic types of surface lures: (1) coverage and (2) target.

• *Coverage* — When fishing open water, grassbeds and flats (or during periods of dropping water levels), it is generally difficult to know where strikes

BIG BASS are attracted to cover, making buzzbaits a plus for fishing in shallow water.

will occur. By using walking stickbaits or buzzbaits (lures that move continuously across the surface), the object is to isolate the type of areas that hold fish.

"If I'm fishing along and catch a decent fish, immediately I'm trying to remember exactly what kind of bank it was, what kind of structure was nearby (chunk rock, pea gravel, etc.), the amount of grass present, anything that might make a difference," notes Rowland. "Then, I try to duplicate as many of those exact same things in other areas."

• *Target lures* — If an area is producing fish from well-defined targets, such as small bushes or flooded willows, the advantage to a coverage lure is diminished. Now, target-oriented lures, like chuggers, can be placed right in the strike zone, right around the target. These areas also include boat docks, laydowns or anything that can be precisely identified as a target zone.

• *Gauging strike zones* — Start with a coverage lure. If strikes are generated off a certain type of cover or structure — and it happens two or three times — then change to a target lure for greater efficiency.

• *Big fish areas* — Big fish tend to be loners and rarely school as compared to smaller fish. These larger individuals also control a small home territory which provides three key ingredients: (1) cover, (2) easily caught forage and (3) ready access to deeper water.

• *Feeding aggressiveness* — According to Tauber, the first strike or two in the morning is a key indicator to the general feeding mood for at least the morning period. This activity level may change later due to high sun or cloudy conditions.

"If your first strike is just a push or a slush, it's not an aggressive strike. And it can indicate the start of a very long, frustrating day. At this point, I'll rig up a Slug-Go or Fat Gitzit as a backup lure. Then, my goal is not necessarily to catch them on the topwater bait, but locate the fish for the backup lure.

"If the first strike is a crunch, you better get on the trolling motor and cover a lot of water, because the fish are trying to tell you they're actively feeding on the surface."

Different retrieve speeds and lure cadences should be used until the most productive ones are determined. Even in colder water, slow speeds may not always be the key to triggering strikes. At times, faster, more abrupt cadences can generate reaction bites.

• *Bait sizes* — "Matching the lure to the forage is as critical to me as jig color is to

Denny Brauer or Tommy Biffle," says Rowland.

"Matching the bait to the forage has a lot to do with observation. If you see a school of shad working in the back of a pocket, you should always make a point to go back amongst that school to get a feel for the size of shad that are in shallow water."

In the early season, smaller baits are generally the rule: Pop-Rs, Ricos, Yo-Zuri chuggers or small minnow-type baits, such as Rapalas, Daiwa TD Minnows or Yo-Zuri Crystal Minnows.

As the water warms and activity increases, use larger, more aggressive, moving baits — such as Zara Spooks, Super Spooks, Crosswalkers, ZZ Tops or Yo-Zuri Walking Sticks.

TOPWATER LIMITATIONS

• *Cover or vegetation* — Thick cover or matted vegetation will often limit or eliminate certain topwater lures from consideration. Versatility with different types of surface baits is crucial.

• *Windy weather* — Although buzzbaits can be effective in windy weather, Tauber insists that strong winds greatly reduce the effectiveness of most topwater offerings. "When you limit the ability of fish to see your lure, you reduce the attractiveness of that lure."

Matching The Lure To The Hit

When he's topwater fishing, veteran BASS pro Larry Nixon decides which topwater lure to use by the type of strike he gets. While it's true that any kind of strike indicates you're doing something right, Nixon studies the way a bass hits to determine whether a slight modification of his lure or retrieve might result in more success.

"If a bass hits very easy, very lightly and not aggressively, I know that a minnow bait, which has a slim profile, is frequently more effective — especially when fished very slowly and deliberately," he explains. "These lures look completely natural in the water, even when fished very slowly."

By contrast, if Nixon gets a huge, explosive strike, it usually means the bass are aggressive. After a strike like this, he speeds up his retrieve, which enables him to cover water more quickly.

"This may be a good time to use a walking bait, like a Zara Spook, a Spit'n King, or a Chug Bug, because you can really work them fast and create a lot of commotion," says Nixon. "If you're in big bass water, you might even change to a larger lure to try to attract one of the larger fish.

"One of the presentations I like to use for aggressive bass is a jumping/skipping retrieve that excites the fish and triggers a reflex strike. I move the lure as rapidly as possible because I don't want them to get a good look at it; I think they're striking just because my lure invaded their territory."

One misconception many anglers have is that if bass are suspended over extremely deep water, it will take a very loud and noisy topwater plug to make them come to the surface.

"Overall, I think the cadence or speed of your retrieve is more important," he explains. "Remember, even though you may be fishing water 50 feet deep, the bass are probably suspended only 10 to 15 feet down. They hear your lure the instant it touches the surface.

"Charlie Campbell and some of the topwater pros who fish Table Rock and Bull Shoals often demonstrate this when they throw a topwater plug out into some of the open coves and just wallow it slowly but steadily across the surface. Sometimes they're fishing water 100 feet deep, but bass come up and absolutely blast those plugs. Only the slow, steady retrieve works in this situation, however. If you try to work the lure fast, or even with a stop-and-go presentation, the fish generally don't pay any attention to it."

PERFECT PLUGS

They spit, sputter and dive —
knowing how to choose
the right topwater is the key . . .

ZELL ROWLAND'S POP-R MAGIC

This Texas pro's money bait is an old-fashioned chugger, fished with finesse

A SIMPLE BAIT THAT almost faded into obscurity, the Pop-R was revived, thanks to the success of several professional anglers. Chief among them is veteran Zell Rowland, who has nearly made an angling career out of his favorite lure — the Pop-R.

Representative of a long list of chuggers, the cigar-shaped plug with a concave mouth is a surface lure designed to push water while making its characteristic plopping sound.

Zell Rowland's exploits include winning a June event held on Tennessee's Lake Chickamauga, where he proved that topwaters could draw strikes all day long, sun or no sun. More Pop-R success came with a near victory in the 1991 Bassmaster Classic, which he led for two days.

Why so much confidence in a single lure? According to Rowland, it's all in the lure's unique sound. "It sounds exactly like a shad flicking on the surface of the water," he suggests. And for bass foraging on shad, that's like ringing the dinner bell.

HOW AND WHERE TO POP

Rowland says the key to success depends more on *where* you put the bait than how you retrieve it.

Grass and rock lead his list of favorite types of cover. "Grass is best because of the number of fish it can hold," he speculates. "Rock, on the other hand, is more defined and usually holds fewer active fish."

When fishing grassbeds, he first tries the contour edges, and then probes the interiors looking for holes, cuts and pockets.

Rock requires a different strategy. "Usually, a rock pattern will only give up one or two fish in a given spot," he contends. "Whether I'm fishing riprap or rocky points, I try to find lots of spots that will give up a fish or two. It's an all-day pattern, but it can add up!"

Flooded brush ranks low on Rowland's list of

Topwater Tips

PRADCO, maker of the Rebel Pop-R, had just quit production on its Pop-R popper when Texas angler Zell Rowland's successes with the bait created a groundswell of demand. Rowland's ability to make the lure "spit" on retrieve overcame any inhibitions bass may have had about striking the lure. To mimic his technique, start with the rod tip at the 10 o'clock position, and twitch upward to move the bait 6 to 12 inches per pull. As the lure nears the boat, lower the rod tip, eventually to the water's surface, and continue the short, rhythmic twitches of the rod tip.

(Opposite page)
ZELL ROWLAND
begins working a
Pop-R with a quick
cadence. He then
progressively slows
the presentation until
locking in on a strike
pattern.

ZELL ROWLAND prefers a medium-light action rod for Pop-Rs because it's forgiving enough to hook scrappy fish on the small treble hook.

preferred habitat for chugging. He tries other baits for brush, unless he is in a clear reservoir that has brush as its primary cover.

Retrieve speed depends on several factors, including water clarity, temperature and mood of the fish. Rowland likes a fast retrieve — a continuous, rhythmic pace with an occasional pause — if conditions allow. Start fast, and then slow the pace until you find what the fish want.

He casts slightly beyond his target, engages the reel and begins twitching the rod tip. He holds the rod at the 10 o'clock position first, gradually lowering the tip as the bait nears the boat. With each pull, the lure should travel approximately 6 to 12 inches, spitting water nearly that distance in front of its concave mouth.

Lethargic or deep-holding fish, such as those in stained or cold water, call for a slower pace. Try shorter pulls and longer pauses, he suggests, especially if the water's dingy or cool.

To execute his technique, Rowland employs a 6 1/2-foot trigger-style casting rod in a medium-light action. The soft tip serves two purposes: It has just the right response to move the bait correctly, and it's forgiving enough to help land scrappy fish on the small treble. His line choices run from 12- to 20-pound test (12 for slower retrieves and 20 for quicker speeds or around thick cover).

Another advantage to these surface lures is their ability to draw fish from great

Rowland's Chugger Checklist

■ **Lure** — Rebel Pop-R, Heddon Chugger, Pico Pop, The Shape's Michael, Lobina Lures' Rico, Poe's Blurpee, Cordell Near-Nuthin', Bomber Popper.
■ **Equipment** — 12- and 20-pound monofilament, 6 1/2-foot medium-light trigger-style casting rod (graphite), bass-size casting reel.
■ **Seasonal Effectiveness** — Prespawn through late fall. Very effective on schooling bass.
■ **Water Temperature** — Lower 60s to 80s.
■ **Water Clarity** — Clear to at least 1 1/2 foot visibility; not particularly effective in stained water.
■ **Cover/Structure** — Grass is best (submerged or emergent). Rocks also (riprap, rocky bluffs or points, pea gravel banks, etc.) can be good.
■ **Depth Range** — Most effective when fish are within 5 feet of surface, but can draw them from extreme depths of 15 feet or more.
■ **Presentation** — Long casts are best in clear water. During retrieve, hold rod tip up (10 o'clock) at first, then lower as bait draws near.
■ **Cadence** — Steady, rhythmic twitches of the rod tip, making the lure slide and pop on the surface approximately 6 to 12 inches per twitch. Start fast, then slow down cadence until contact is made with fish.

Pop-R Workshop

Zell Rowland's workshop is not very big and doesn't have a lot of expensive tools, but the lures he fashions there are world famous. He receives correspondence and even visitors from throughout the United States who want to learn his magic, and some of his lures have been auctioned for prices as high as $600.

Surprisingly, this Texas pro doesn't make new lures; instead, his fame comes from the modifications he makes to existing ones, specifically, the Pop-R.

"What I do to the Pop-R is simply make it a more efficient lure for the way I want to fish it," says Rowland.

"Topwater lures are really more versatile than most anglers realize, and by changing the Pop-R, I can add to that versatility."

The first step is removing the hooks and sanding the lure. Rowland does this by hand, not only removing all the paint but also getting the sides completely smooth. He uses 100- to 150-grit sandpaper, and often counts the number of strokes per side to ensure better balance. Very little sanding is done on the bottom; most is on the sides and top.

distances. "I've seen them charge a bait from a depth of 25 feet in the crystal waters out west," he claims. This can be the case if you are subjected to suspended fish along bluff walls in deep, clear reservoirs — a situation that renders most lures useless.

In short, the Pop-R is a deadly surface lure with the ability to produce fish all day. Remember to start with a quick cadence, then slow down until a fish hits. By following these instructions, you, too, can master the Pop-R, the lure that simulates sounds of a shad on the run.

"The smooth sides reduce the Pop-R's resistance in the water," says Rowland. "The lure moves more freely and reacts better and faster. Normally, I spend about two hours on the small Pop-R, a little longer on the medium one. The final sanding is with a fine emery cloth."

Contrary to what many have heard and tried themselves, Rowland does not sand down the lower lip of the lure's concave face. He does, however, sand around the outside of the face to produce a sharper, finer edge.

"Sanding around the face changes the shape from round to oval and changes how the lure sounds when it comes through the water," Rowland explains. "Many fishermen say a Pop-R's effectiveness comes when it 'spits' water each time you pop it, but I don't care if it spits water or not.

"What I want is the sound the lure makes each time I work it."

The next step is painting, which is done with a small hand-held sprayer, but the paint is anything but ordinary. Rowland and his close friend, well-known Conroe, Texas, taxidermist Al Hillmeyer, spend hours mixing special paint concoctions that are far more accurate and lifelike than anything coming out of a factory.

"There are times when sight is the primary key that triggers a bass into striking a topwater lure," Rowland notes, "so I want my lure to appear as natural as possible. At the same time, by hand-painting my own lures, I know no one else I'm competing against has the same color, so it may give me a slight edge."

After painting both the lure body and the eyes, Rowland applies a final clear coating, almost like a syrup glaze, that adds shine to the lure.

The final step is tying chicken feathers around the rear treble hook.

"Feathers are more lifelike than bucktail," says Rowland, "because they breathe better, literally opening and closing as the lure is worked.

"I match my colors carefully. My favorite combinations are white, red/white, yellow/white, blue/white, and chartreuse/white. Tying the feathers is absolutely critical, too" he adds, "even though it only takes a minute or two.

"I use six feathers on my hooks, and all are the same length. That way, they open and close like a flower. If I start getting a lot of short strikes, I simply shorten the feathers."

Just how good is one of Rowland's hand-finished lures when compared to an off-the-shelf Pop-R? Those who have the modified lures say there's no comparison; Rowland himself once outfished a friend using a standard Pop-R, 75 bass to three.

"I like throwing a lure I know isn't just like the lures used by everyone else," says Rowland. "The only way to get that is to do it myself."

THE ART AND CRAFT OF FISHING ZARA SPOOKS

This cigar-shaped stickbait has no action of its own, but in the hands of a master, it's irresistible to big bass

WHEN YOU GET right down to it, bass fishing is not the most graceful sport. For pure visual beauty, chunkin' and windin' cannot compete with the smooth, graceful casts of the fly rodder.

Still, some lure presentations are pleasing to watch — the fluid motion of an expert flipper who has found his "groove," for example.

Of the thousands of techniques common to bass angling, certainly the manipulation of the classic Heddon Zara Spook is one of the most artful. With nothing more than a few well-timed jerks of the rod tip, a skilled angler can breathe life into a mere piece of plastic.

In the hands of an expert, a Spook will obey its master's commands as obediently as the finest bird dog. And because the lure has no innate action, any movement it might make is a direct result of the fisherman tugging on its tether. The lure literally becomes an extension of the angler himself.

WALKING THE DOG

Though these plugs can be worked in a variety of fashions, one particular technique is virtually synonymous with the Zara Spook. "Walking the dog," as it is commonly called, causes the plug to swish back and forth in a zigzag motion. A proficient Spook angler can walk the bait back and forth with so little forward motion that it appears as if the bait is simply swimming of its own ac-

Topwater Tips

The Zara Spook and similar stickbaits come by their name honestly — they look like nothing more than a stick floating on the water. When you call them into action with the rhythmic twitch that makes them come alive, they resemble an injured baitfish sloshing on the surface. But sometimes, bass seem to prefer a "dead" stickbait. Especially in the clear smallmouth lakes of the North Country, anglers have found that they can catch huge smallmouth by twitching the bait a few times, then letting it sit still on the surface — sometimes for as long as a minute. Strange, but true.

cord in one tiny area. In fact, a true master can stretch a single cast into a breathtaking 10 minute adventure in which a strike is likely to occur at any moment.

Basil Bacon, a veteran BASS pro from the Missouri Ozarks, has been Spook fishing for 30 years and is widely regarded as one of the finest Zara Spook masters in the sport.

Walking the dog is accomplished by creating a cadence with short jerks of the rod tip while incorporating slack line offerings and slight cranks of the reel handle. When asked to relate the procedure, Bacon provided the following instructions.

"The rod tip is always pointed down toward the water, and the technique is easier if you will palm your baitcasting reel. The real key to walking the dog is keeping slack in the line, and then jerking the slack out of the line rather than jerking the plug itself. Personally, I try to keep 12 to 18 inches of slack in my line at all times.

"The retrieve is basically a cadence based on intervals of about half a second. Something like jerk — slack — jerk — slack. When you jerk the slack out of the line, that causes the bait's nose to swing around to the opposite side, but then you have to give the bait slack line so it can turn around freely and unencumbered. Really, that's all there is to it. The only other thing you must do," Bacon says, "is learn how far to crank the reel handle in order to take up the correct amount of line. If you take up too much line, the bait will move toward you rather than swimming side to side."

AVOID USING heavier line than 14-pound test because it will adversely affect the action of a Zara Spook.

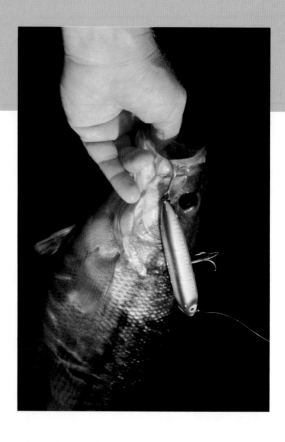

Varying a Spook's retrieve is usually accomplished by increasing or decreasing the speed and/or frequency at which the plug swims back and forth. For example, an angler who is slowly walking the dog might make the bait swim lazily back and forth so that each movement to the side is a long, slow, delicate glide. A fast paced retrieve, on the other hand, might cause the Spook to zip rapidly to and fro in short, quick skips so that the plug throws a spray of water each time it changes direction.

To achieve optimum performance from the Spook, an angler must use equipment that is matched to the task.

"A good 5 1/2-foot rod can actually do 90 percent of the work for you," says Bacon. "You need a soft, light action tip to make the plug work properly, but it needs to be mated with a stout backbone since you so often catch big fish on a Spook."

Line size is an important consideration when fishing Spooks, Bacon believes. He chooses 14-pound test, noting that a lighter line will allow the lure to swing too far to the side, thereby allowing the line to foul in the hooks. A heavier line, on the other hand, produces too much drag for the lure to overcome and it will not be able to swing far enough to the side. "And if your line is kinked or coiled," Basil says, "it won't work with a Spook. Those kinks act just like a spring, and they won't let the bait pull any slack so that it can turn to the side."

DEEP BLUFF BANKS are prime areas for using the Zara Spook in postspawn.

SPOOKS THROUGH THE SEASONS

Astute anglers have learned that, unlike many other topwater plugs, Spooks are capable of catching fish virtually year-round in the southern half of the United States, while they serve admirably as three-season lures in the Northern waters.

Tennessean Sonny Fletcher has been a rabid Spook thrower for three decades and counting. Fletcher's Spook fishing

CLEAR-HUED SPOOKS are best in clear water. Darker colors, like bullfrog, are geared for dingy conditions.

usually picks up in February when the bass in Tennessee first start easing into the shallows. "From then until April, I'll concentrate on long, shallow points that are close to deep water. I use a slow, steady retrieve with very little forward progress," he reports.

As the fish migrate back into the coves, creeks and pockets in search of spawning grounds and warmer water, Fletcher follows. "From then until the postspawn period, I'll be looking for shallow water structures and spawning areas."

In the immediate postspawn period, Fletcher targets bluff banks that drop into 40 or 50 feet of water, recognizing the bass' tendency to suspend just after the spawn.

"I personally feel that the Zara Spook really shines as a topwater bait from postspawn on through the summer," Fletcher says, "because it will literally bring to the surface bass that are suspending in 50 feet of water or holding on deep structure."

From that point on through September, Fletcher concentrates on deep structure, patiently working his Spook far above the fish in an effort to lure them to the surface.

He concentrates on grassbeds in 20 to 25 feet of water when fishing slack water, but also works bridge pilings and submerged humps in current-laden rivers. Bacon focuses on channel breaks, ledges and deep points.

While Fletcher says Spooks are productive throughout a summer's day, Bacon believes they work best early, late and at noon.

"These plugs are great when the sun is directly overhead," Bacon says. "The reason, I think, is that when the sun is directly overhead, Spooks create a superb silhouette that the fish can see easily through the depths."

In the fall, both experts gradually move from main lake structures to the back ends of coves and creeks, roughly following the migration of the bass as the fish follow the shad.

Through the winter months, the anglers pick up a Spook whenever they locate fish in relatively shallow water.

"After a few days of warm, sunny weather, Spooks will pull bass to the surface even though the water temperature might be in the 40s," Fletcher says. Understandably, these plugs will rarely draw strikes from lethargic, deep water bass during the coldest months of the year.

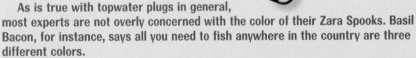

Spook Tips And Tactics

As is true with topwater plugs in general, most experts are not overly concerned with the color of their Zara Spooks. Basil Bacon, for instance, says all you need to fish anywhere in the country are three different colors.

"You need something with a flash to it — like chrome — for use in clear water, something with a white belly to use in dingy water, and then something reminiscent of a perch — like a perch, bullfrog or yellow shore minnow pattern — to use in the northern states."

For the most part, Sonny Fletcher agrees, adding, "The clear Spook is probably best for clear water, but it is so hard to see that I rarely use it. Chrome, or one of the silver G-finish plugs, seems to do the job just fine."

For some reason, bass often swirl, bump or swipe their tail at Spooks, and big smallmouth seem to be particularly notorious for it.

Fletcher believes that when the bass are rolling at the Spook, as so often happens, they are simply trying to scare it away.

"Sometimes, if you switch colors, the bass will start biting the plug. If a color switch doesn't work, I'll change to the downsized Zara Puppy, and that tends to work especially well in the spring."

Knowing when to set the hook is always a concern when fishing topwater plugs, and Spooks are no exception.

"You cannot set the hook until you actually feel the fish on the line," Bacon says. "But there's not a man in the world who can keep from setting the hook the instant a giant bass explodes on a Spook. You'll probably miss that fish, but you can't really help it!"

For optimum action, Fletcher recommends tying the Spook to your line using some type of hanging loop. Furthermore, he always adds split rings between his Zara's hook hangers and hooks. "The immovable hangers on a Zara will give the fish something to twist against, and I honestly believe the addition of split rings has cut my number of lost fish in half."

BAITS WITH PROPS

Sometimes you have to force yourself to use propeller plugs

I F THE NIKE CORP. made fishing lures and not athletic shoes, its advertising admonition of "Just do it" would lose none of its meaning — especially if they were referring to prop baits.

Neither fish nor fowl in the world of topwater lures, prop baits don't have amnesia — fishermen forget about them. Even the most diligent angler seems to forget about them. As a result, questions of where to use them, when to use them or how to use them are often outweighed by a subtle but simple unwillingness to "just do it."

With spinning props at one or both ends and a shape that often resembles a minnow lure, prop baits look more like refugees from a vintage lure catalog. To some anglers, they just may not seem like serious baits.

Most likely, the reason for angler indifference comes with the middle ground these lures occupy in topwater strategy. Instead of holding a recognizable niche, prop baits do a lot of things well, but none as flashy or brilliantly as other surface lures.

Being more target-oriented, they are not the optimum choice for a fast moving, search bait scenario. Nor do they seem to draw fish from greater distances. So why use them?

To answer that question, perhaps anglers should listen to Zell Rowland, the one man among the professional ranks to truly build a career on his topwater mastery.

"In the spring, I don't need to tell a fisherman where to fish. When I ask them, 'Where?' they'll tell me, 'Shallow water.' When I ask, 'Why?' they tell me, 'Because the fish are on the bank.' Then, when I ask, 'If a bush is on the bank, do you think your odds of catching a bass would be better?' the answer will be, 'Absolutely.' "

Clearly, what Rowland is saying goes right to the heart of most shallow water fishing

(Opposite page) IF A WALKING BAIT or chugger is not producing, then making the switch to prop baits is the next best move.

Topwater Tips

Topwaters — especially those with a propeller at one or both ends — are effective medicine in fast moving rivers and streams. Cast a prop bait into an eddy behind a boulder or logjam and let it sit briefly. Before the current drags the line and lure out of the eddy, twitch the bait sharply to make the props spin — and hold on. The baits are similarly effective when cast upstream and across the current. Pull them 12 to 24 inches at a time, then let them bob in the riffles for several feet. Smallmouth, spotted bass and largemouth all love prop baits in moving water.

PROP BAITS ARE effective anytime bass are relating to shallow cover, such as dock pilings.

situations: When the fish are on the bank and the shallows are littered with targets, a target-oriented lure seems like a very smart choice. This is particularly true when a bait has the ability to stay in the strike zone longer, yet still produce its strike-generating action. So far, nothing has been mentioned that doesn't apply to prop baits.

To take the discussion one step further, what if these same lures offered an erratic, surface-splashing display that combines the best attributes of several lures? Is that such a bad thing?

In this world of specialization, some might argue — and perhaps accurately — that such a combination of attributes is precisely what keeps prop baits from finding greater favor. No argument there. To honestly have confidence in any lure, an angler must recognize its strengths and be able to take advantage of them.

First and foremost, Rowland looks to prop baits when his goal is to produce more disturbance in the water. Most often, this is when a chop or ripple guides him to a bait that can get noticed. In this instance, his choice would be a two-prop model, such as the venerable Devil's Horse.

However, when getting noticed is also required in calm conditions, Rowland turns to single-prop versions, like the Heddon Tiny Torpedo. More of

a finesse lure than a power bait, these single-prop lures provide even more options when it comes to action. With the prop on the back, the lure sits tail-down in the water, making it very easy to walk from side to side, like a Zara Spook.

As with any lure, determining whether the fish want a certain action and then how they want it demands precisely the same trial-and-error work. The beauty of prop baits is that shoreline cover offers a wealth of possibilities — exactly the kinds of targets where these baits excel.

As previously mentioned, trying to narrow down the best times for props may be the biggest reason fishermen end up not using them at all. But, if you have to make some tough decisions, remember that the target-oriented nature of these lures makes them a first choice when bass are less willing to chase and more comfortable sticking close to cover. If a walking bait or chugger is not producing or, at best, only drawing half-hearted responses, then props may be the key.

In the spring, after bass have spawned and start to ease off the bank, Rowland finds that prop bait action is deadly on fish that are feeding on fry or shad. To him, these bass want a lure that moves, and prop baits fill the bill on all counts.

"If I'm doing subtle little blurps, I do them in a

very quick cadence. I'm moving the bait anywhere from 2 to 4 feet. Then there are times when I rip it, sweeping the rod and moving it 4 or 5 feet at a time. Other times, I'll work the lure so it barely has any forward movement."

It should be noted that it is very easy to overwork a prop bait. The triggering motion is often very subtle, so it takes an observant angler to know exactly what created the strike.

While spring offers some of the best conditions for shallow bass around cover, Rowland warns against pigeonholing these lures. Anytime bass are relating to shallow cover — such as dock pilings or weed edges in the summer and fall — prop baits can be effective.

For other bass species, like smallmouth, the target areas will shift from cover to rocky flats. Another change may come in the depth being fished, since the generally clearer water found in smallmouth situations will easily draw fish up in areas 5 to 6 feet deep.

"With any species of bass, the presentation of the lure is more erratic than any of the other topwater baits. It's almost an action like you would work a Zara Spook, which means you're constantly moving the bait and creating a disturbance.

"But there are times when the fish are hitting it and not getting it, so I'll add a feather trailer to a prop bait. When I add the feather trailer, I can work the lure slower and still have a lot of action just because of what that trailer does for that slow speed presentation."

Prop Bait Theory

Prop baits fall into two basic categories:
• Floating lures with propellers at both ends — These baits float evenly at rest.
• Floating lures with propellers at one end, usually the tail — These baits often sit at a 45 to 90 degree angle at rest, with the tail submerged.

Propeller baits are among the oldest bass lure designs.

"Prop baits were among the most common early bass lures, probably because they were relatively simple to make," believes Barry Stegall of Bomber Lures. "Many were just a simple stick with spinners on the ends. But the design has stayed viable for two reasons: Prop baits work, and they're fun to use."

Simple, yes, but there are subtle complexities that can determine whether a prop bait draws strikes or merely moves water.

"With these lures, the propellers are the key components," according to Dan Wyatt. The Carthage, Mo., lure manufacturer knows that it takes the right prop design to make them work correctly. "Just as it takes the right prop to make your bass boat perform properly, a prop bait must have the proper prop to run right."

Just as with a boat or aircraft propeller, a prop bait's propeller must have the right pitch for optimum performance.

"When you were a kid, you probably stuck your hand out the car window and felt the varying degrees of force exerted by the wind velocity as you rotated your palm," he explains. "With the palm held flat against the wind, the force felt like it would jerk your arm off. If you tilted your hand sharply, the force of the wind was greatly reduced."

Wyatt says the same principle applies to the propeller on a lure. "If you had a perfectly flat prop, one with no twist, it would have zero pitch. Trying to fish a lure with one or two props like this would be like trying to haul a flat board through the water. There would be too much resistance. But if the prop blades were set to slice through the water like a razor blade, the lure wouldn't work because there wouldn't be enough water resistance to turn the blades."

"Our prop baits, including the Woodchopper and Wood Popper, use a 'maximum-pitch' prop," explains Dan's brother, Phil Wyatt. "We feel there's an optimum pitch, a point where the lure's performance is just right. Any more pitch, and the props wouldn't rotate properly. Any less pitch, and too much water would flow over the blades, again causing improper rotation."

Bomber's Barry Stegall says, "A pitch that is too high on the prop will cause the lure to roll. It's like trying to turn a 30-pitch prop with a 150-hp engine: you just can't do it." Stegall, like many anglers, claims he can tell when a prop bait is working right by listening to it. "I want it to gurgle or sputter," he says. "If you catch a lot of fish on it, the lure may get a little out of tune. When that happens, bend or twist the blades with your fingers or pliers, in opposite directions."

Besides their characteristic sound, prop baits attract bass visually by throwing water as they're moved.

"The water splash is caused by a combination of the velocity of the prop's rotation and the forward motion exerted against the lure as the fisherman retrieves it," says Wyatt. "A lot of engineering is involved in these baits. You need the right combination of resistance to the water and ease of forward movement to make them look and sound right."

BRINGING UP BASS ON A BABY

These short, fat prop baits work magic when warmwater bass want a topwater lure with finesse

LOOK INSIDE DENNY BRAUER'S rod locker, and you'll find it crammed with heavy-duty baitcasting outfits, each with a jig tied to the line. Almost lost under that mass of stiff rods is a less imposing baitcaster with, of all things, a Heddon Baby Torpedo affixed.

Larry Nixon's collection is a little more varied. You'll see rods adorned with worms, spinnerbaits, crankbaits and jigs. Among that rabble of rods, however, is one with a Baby Torpedo hanging from a guide.

While river smallmouth fanciers and farm pond largemouth specialists have high praise for the various sizes of Torpedos, few lake bass hunters fully recognize their value.

The lineup of Torpedos, which look like short, fat, half-smoked cigars with a propeller attached, include the 1/8-ounce Teeny Torpedo, 1/4-ounce Tiny Torpedo and 3/8-ounce Baby Torpedo.

(Opposite page)
TOP PROS Larry Nixon and Denny Brauer emphasize that prop baits like the Baby Torpedo are vastly underutilized.

Topwater Tips

How do you know whether to fish the larger Baby Torpedo or the downsized Tiny version? It's easy — if bass are hitting the Baby well enough, stay with it. You're likely to catch bigger fish with the plug. If not, drop down to the Tiny Torpedo and see if that makes a difference. Generally, the Tiny will draw more strikes, particularly in challenging situations such as clear water, lakes experiencing lots of fishing pressure, and following a drastic change in the weather or drop in water temperature. Baby Torpedos are recommended in windy, choppy conditions, when the additional noise provided by a bigger propeller is more likely to attract a fish or two.

Ignoring the baits is a big mistake, says veteran BASS pro Brauer, who notes that the Baby Torpedo can fill a very important niche for a lake largemouth fisherman. "The three topwaters I primarily fish are a Rebel Pop-R, a Zara Spook and a buzzbait; each offers the bass a different look and a different action," he explains. "I use the Baby as a change of pace from the Pop-R. These days, so many people throw a chugger that, on highly pressured lakes, especially during the summer, the bait loses some of its appeal. That's the main time I will turn to a Baby."

Nixon, who, along with Brauer, is a million dollar winner on the BASS circuit, agrees with him on those points. But Nixon insists that the bait has other charms as well.

"The main advantage of the Baby Torpedo is that its small profile doesn't create a lot of noise,

which makes it a fantastic lure for bass recuperating from the spawn," he says. "For example, when postspawn bass are spooky and just starting to feed, particularly on small bream and baitfish fry, the Baby closely imitates the low-key commotion these prey fish make on the surface.

"I also like the Baby because it is one of the more buoyant topwaters and sits so high on the water. Give it a little twitch and it bobs right back up."

Brauer has found that a chugger's spitting action — so deadly at times — can be a turnoff when warmwater bass just don't want something so lively. In contrast, the Torpedo is a "finesse topwater bait" that simulates the appearance of a smaller shad or minnow emitting its last death throbs.

To create that illusion, Brauer gently rocks the Baby a couple of times, lets it sit for a few seconds, and then twitches it several more times. The pro emphasizes that, often, the longer your patience can allow this artificial to remain motionless between twitches, the greater your chances of receiving a strike.

Nixon's standard retrieve is slightly more aggressive; he uses a jerk-jerk-jerk-pause gambit. Only rarely does he give the prop bait a hard rip, and only then as a last-ditch tactic.

TIME AND PLACE FOR A BABY

The precise times, places and water conditions to work a Torpedo are other important considerations.

"As river and pond fishermen will tell you, a Torpedo of any kind is a

STREAM ANGLERS recognize that Torpedoes are deadly during the early morning or late evening.

ANGLERS CAN ALTER the action of Torpedoes by bending the prop.

super lure for early morning or late evening during warmwater periods. The same holds true on major impoundments," says Brauer. "And, as is true on rivers and ponds, Torpedos work best when the water is clear or only lightly stained.

"I also like Babys on warm, humid, cloudy days when the bass stop hitting Pop-Rs or buzzbaits. And schooling bass at any time of the day will absolutely eat a Baby Torpedo. In fact, under those two conditions, this lure will catch bass from postspawn all the way into fall."

Except for schooling fish, Brauer regards the Baby Torpedo as a position bait, meaning that he never casts it into open water. Instead, he tosses it near isolated patches of grass, the sides of boat docks, the ends of bluffs, and along weedlines. He believes the lure is simply not a good choice when an angler desires to draw bass up from deep structure or cover, or when the water is extremely stained.

Nixon says the Baby performs best when worked around weedy habitat such as milfoil, hydrilla and lily pads and around visible wood cover, such as stumps that are partially above water.

It is interesting that while Brauer primarily uses the prop bait to imitate the death throbs of a single creature, Nixon employs one to simulate the foraging of a very tiny school of young baitfish.

"A Baby Torpedo moving across the surface creates a little 'buzz' that looks like a small group of baitfish feeding on top," he says. "If you have really still, slick water conditions, the Baby can give the impression of one of these little schools moving along the surface."

However, Nixon ties on a Baby to milk every advantage from a topwater bite.

"Many times you can start off catching surface-feeding school bass with a chugger," he says. "But the longer the feed goes on, and as some of the fish are caught, the bass sometimes stop chasing the Pop-R. The Baby is a position bait that you can leave in the strike zone much longer. That little 'whiz-whiz' noise of the Baby is a good change from the steady, plop-plop of the chugger, and it can result in fish you normally wouldn't catch."

BABY TACKLE

Brauer insists that anglers should avoid pairing stiff rods with Baby Torpedos. He prefers a 6-foot, 3-inch medium-light action baitcaster with a "loose" tip, such as the Daiwa George Cochran Topwater/Twitchin' Rod.

He selects relatively light 12-pound-test line with that outfit, enabling the long casts frequently necessary in the clear water conditions in which the prop bait excels.

Nixon selects the 5 1/2-foot Daiwa V.I.P. fiberglass baitcaster because its soft tip and action "gives the bait to the bass instead of taking it away from them." Nixon also likes this short rod because he prefers to work the lure with the rod tip down and held about 6 inches above the water. While Brauer, who is taller, can get away with a longer rod, Nixon says he would be slapping the water continually with a rod over 6 feet.

HARD MINNOWS are not weedless but can be fished around shoreline cover with excellent results.

HARD MINNOWS are not weedless but can be fished around shoreline cover with excellent results.

FOOLING BASS WITH FAKE MINNOWS

Topwaters that mimic live minnows are time-tested bass baits

THE SLENDER SURFACE lures that mimic minnows took the bass fishing market by storm in the '60s after they were introduced by Rapala. It didn't take long for fishermen who tried them to prove they were as productive as advertised. These lures are often called "twitch baits" because of the twitch-pause-twitch retrieve so commonly used with them. They can be fished in a number of ways to draw strikes from keeper-size bass as well as lunkers.

HARD MINNOW REVIEW

Minnow lures made of wood or hard plastic have been in use by bass anglers since the early 1960s, when the balsa-wood Rapala migrated to the United States from Finland. The Rebel minnow, a design similar to the Rapala but with plastic construction, followed soon after and was also an instant success. Over the years, minnow lures have proved to be consistent sellers; besides the ones mentioned, other popular surface minnows include the Smithwick Rattlin' Rogue, A.C. Shiner, Bagley Bang-O-Lure, Bomber Long A, Cordell Red Fin, Storm Thunderstick and Poe's Cruise Minnow.

All of these lures vary in minor ways, but all have the following in common:

• *Long, slender profile* — Many bass experts believe one of the main reasons these lures are so productive is that they look like a live soft-rayed baitfish, such as a golden shiner or threadfin shad. Soft-rayed forage fish have a long, slender profile and are swallowed easily by bass. Bass learn to avoid eating fish that

(Opposite page) FLASHY HARD MINNOWS are tough to beat on sunny days.

Topwater Tips

Fishermen in Florida lakes, and other waters where clear water enables spotting bass beds, have found a lethal application for minnow lures — catching spawning bass. Most "sight fishermen" prefer tubes, jigs and small worms they can place in the center of a nest and wait for the bass to move the intruder away. But you'll get a different reaction from a bass that spots a minnow bait hovering over the bed. Try this: Cast a twitch bait, such as this baby-bass-pattern Bagley Bang-O-Lure, just past the bed. Slowly pull the lure until it reaches the far edge of the nest and let it lie still. Twitch it slightly, making the bait dive nose-down toward the bottom. If that doesn't bring a strike, wait several seconds — as long as a minute — and repeat.

TOPWATER CLASSICS

Few anglers have fished more surface lures for more hours than Charlie Campbell. Here, the topwater legend describes his favorites

I T IS A WARM SUMMER NIGHT in 1938, and the gently moving water of Missouri's Cowskin Creek feels pleasantly cool to the 5-year-old boy holding on to his father's belt as they wade downstream.

They are bass fishing with steel rods and crochet thread, and the only lure the boy has is a black wooden Arbogast Jitterbug. But it is enough, because both the bass and the goggle-eye perch are biting well.

Skip forward three years, and the boy is old enough to fish alone. He rides his bicycle the three miles from his home to that same Cowskin Creek. Parking the bike, he fishes the five-mile stretch between the two highway bridges with the same black Jitterbug, then hitchhikes back to his bicycle.

(Opposite page) CHARLIE CAMPBELL was one of the first Americans to use a Rapala minnow plug. An original like the one he is holding rented for $25 a day.

In the ensuing years, the young fisherman worked as a guide on Bull Shoals and Table Rock lakes, during which time he was among the first anglers in America to use a new minnow-shaped plug made by a foreign company named Rapala. He went on to design his own topwater lures and redesign others.

He qualified for bass fishing's world championship on five occasions, and has long been considered king of topwater anglers by his peers. Today, Charlie Campbell still fishes BASS tournaments — often with topwater lures.

"When I was young, we used topwater plugs because there weren't any large impoundments, and the rivers and creeks we fished were shallow," he explains. "It was so much fun seeing a big bass come up and smash your lure that some of us never stopped fishing topwaters."

Topwater Tips

The Heddon Lucky 13 is a product of the Golden Age of Topwaters. The mere mention of its name brings smiles to longtime bass anglers who remember magic moments when they used it. They are surprisingly versatile, providing the benefits of a floater/diver plug and a chugger. A sharp twitch brings a resounding "bloop," while a slower pull causes it to dive under water. They're great "target" baits, meaning they're designed more for casting to the edge of cover and working in a confined area — as opposed to covering broad sections of water, like a stickbait. In the age of Pop-Rs, Chug Bugs and similar modern poppers, Lucky 13s have been all but forgotten. Try one next time you go topwater fishing. When you do, remember that the old red head/white body color pattern is as effective today as it was 80 years ago.

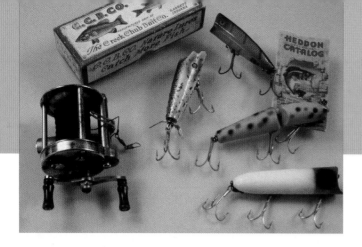

He didn't realize it at the time, of course, but this polite, soft-spoken Missouri pro enjoyed a front-row seat during what had to be the Golden Age of topwater fishing. It was the Golden Age because bass fishing as a sport was still young and the lures themselves were primarily wood, providing an action considerably different from today's plastic.

Some of the lures Campbell fished with for more than three decades — and still uses today — have become classics and highly sought-after collectibles.

Here's what he remembers about some of those famous topwater lures from nearly half a century ago:

HEDDON LUCKY 13

"The original Lucky 13 was a wooden lure about 4 inches long, and it featured a deep concave face and three big treble hooks. It was introduced in the 1920s, and I was using them in the early '50s," says Campbell. "We called them 'two-way' plugs because you could pop them on top, and then pull them underwater because of the face design.

Most Valuable Antique Topwaters

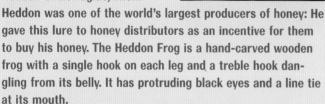

HEDDON FROG $30,000

One of the rarest antique lures in existence today, hence the hefty price tag, this lure was hand-carved in 1897 by James Heddon of Dowagiac, Mich. Heddon was one of the world's largest producers of honey: He gave this lure to honey distributors as an incentive for them to buy his honey. The Heddon Frog is a hand-carved wooden frog with a single hook on each leg and a treble hook dangling from its belly. It has protruding black eyes and a line tie at its mouth.

HEDDON NIGHT RADIANT $10,000

This lure, a Heddon creation of 1912, is a topwater plug with a bloated head and a slender rear. It is finished with luminous paint, and it has a black

stripe from nose to tail. Two double hooks dangle from its head, and a treble hook is in the rear. An all-ivory version of this lure — no stripe — with four trebles is worth about $5,000.

PFLUEGER TRORY MINNOW $10,000

Produced from 1900 to about 1907, this Pflueger model has five treble hooks, and propellers fore and aft. The wooden plug was made in luminous and nonluminous versions.

HEDDON DOWAGIAC MINNOW $10,000

Several versions of this lure are available — at least 15 versions still exist today — ranging in current value from $75 to $10,000. Most models have three or five treble hooks. The Dowagiac Minnow was introduced around 1904 and produced until at least 1930. Heddon named the bait after Dowagiac, Mich., where he lived and made fishing tackle. An original Dowagiac Minnow box can be worth up to $1,500. One version, a Dowagiac Minnow #150, listed in Karl White's, noted antique lure expert, newest book as worth $10,000, actually brought White $48,500 once. The model he had was still in its box and in flawless condition.

THE HEDDON Lucky 13
is another favorite of
Charlie Campbell.

"We also used a smaller version known as the Baby 13, and both lures would catch largemouth and smallmouth. I'd throw into the eddies behind rocks or logs in the creeks and pop the lure three times and then pull it under for a smallmouth, or pop it once and pull it down for a largemouth.

"When I was guiding on the White River, I'd drill holes in the sides of the Baby 13 and glue rubber bands in them just for added action for the smallmouth. Later, after Heddon switched from wood to plastic Lucky 13s, I paid $100 for one of the old wooden ones."

CRAZY CRAWLER

"This lure dates from about 1940, and is still made today, although not in wood like the early ones. It's one of my all-time favorite topwaters, and I still use it regularly when I'm float fishing or fishing at night. All you do is cast it and reel back. The lure makes a clanking sound unlike any other topwater lure."

RAPALA

"In the early 1960s, the owner of a tackle shop in Branson had one floating Rapala

THE HEDDON S.O.S.
Wounded Minnow,
introduced in 1927,
featured a slightly
curved body that
made the lure swim
to one side.

HEDDON UNDERWATER EXPERT $9,000

This Heddon lure was made in 1890. It is 4 1/4 inches long and has five treble hooks, and a propeller in the front. Its

cousin (shown), worth $7,000, was made in 1904. It's 2 1/2 inches long, is bright white with gold trim, and has three treble hooks, and a propeller in front.

MOONLIGHT DREADNOUGHT $5,000

This lure, made in 1918 by Moonlight Bait Co., has a half-red, half-white body with five treble

hooks, and propellers at the head and rear. It was named after a type of early 1900s British battleship.

HARDY INTERCHANGEABLE MINNOW $5,000

Made in 1907 by W.A. Hardy in Indiana, this lure was America's first bass bait to come with extra bodies so the

angler could change the color of the lure without having to change the entire lure. It has glass eyes, three treble hooks, propellers, and a release harness around the center for changing bodies. Its original box is worth up to $3,000.

UNION SPRINGS SPECIALTY MILLER'S REVERSIBLE MINNOW $5,000

This peculiar lure, made of red cedar, has two multiple-arm spinners — placed between segments of the body — that rotate in opposite directions. It was made in 1916 by W.H. Miller of Union Springs, N.Y., near Cayuga Lake. (Continued on page 56)

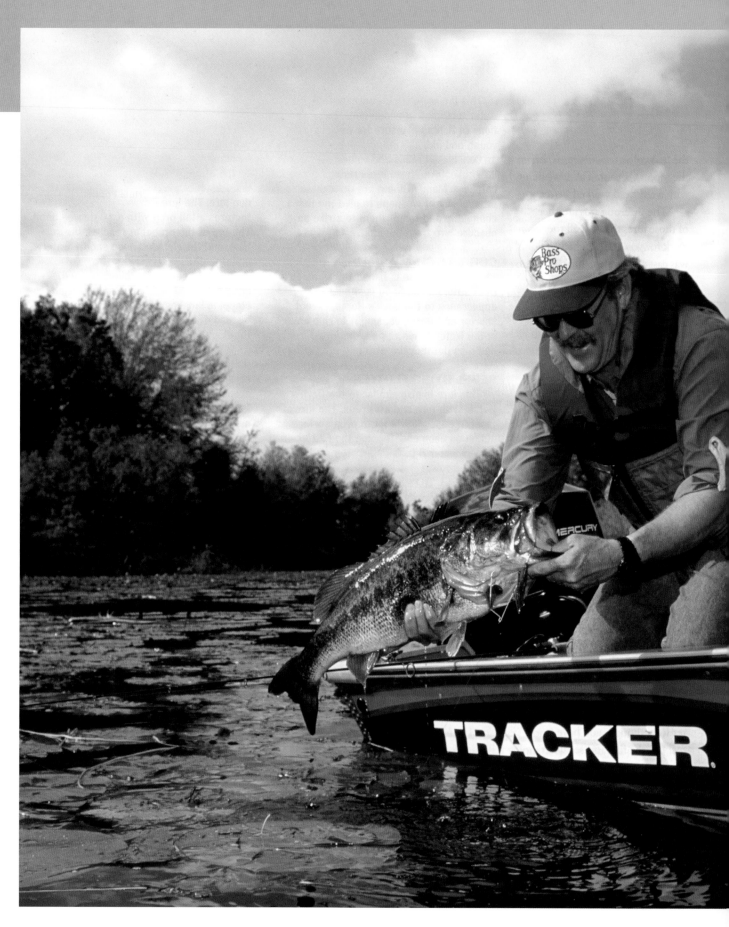

SPOONS & BUZZERS

Use metal topwaters to clack
and sashay across the surface . . .

SKIRTS GIVE topwater spoons added strike appeal when the bite is slow.

SPOONING FOR BASS
This simple metal slab remains a timeless fish-catcher

UNQUESTIONABLY, THE WEEDLESS SPOON is a classic in the lineup of lures. Since the 19th century, weedless spoons have slayed fish, particularly bass. Their unique design allows them to be cast and retrieved where other baits dare not swim. Also, their wobble and flash are particularly seductive to largemouth sulking beneath thick, overhead cover. Truly, weedless spoons have earned their reputation as baits that produce big bass.

Two other classics of bass fishing are Bill Dance and Roland Martin. Both of these legendary anglers credit the weedless spoon for making their careers. To this day, Dance and Martin remain fans of the spoon and fish it whenever the conditions are right.

"You can fish a weedless spoon in places that are impossible to work with other lures, and it maintains its action from the start of the cast until you lift it off the water," Dance describes. "Also, a swimming spoon is a lure for a precise job; there's nothing else like it. So every bass fisherman should have a selection of spoons and the know-how to use them properly."

Adds Martin, "I've caught 37 bass over 10 pounds on black Johnson spoons from the grassbeds of Santee Cooper Reservoir (South Carolina)," Martin recalls of his old guiding waters. "In May 1970, I caught 42 bass over 8 pounds on spoons. In May 1979, I used spoons and caught a 10 fish limit that weighed 89 pounds. I think I could have topped 100 pounds that day, but I lost or tore up all the spoons I had."

(Opposite page) TOPWATER SPOONS come out of Roland Martin's tacklebox when the water temperature reaches 70 degrees.

Topwater Tips

Look at the underside of a weedless spoon, and you'll instantly know where the lure got its name. The curved belly enables it to ride across surface slop and weave through stands of reeds and other cover. Surface spoons generally entice more strikes when they're dressed with a limber trailer, such as a pork frog or plastic grub, or a spinnerbait skirt. For best results, cast across a patch of lily pads or other surface vegetation and reel steadily back. When the lure encounters a hole in the cover, let it sink several inches, then resume the retrieve.

LOCATIONS AND CONDITIONS

Designed for sliding over or swimming through thick cover that other lures have difficulty penetrating, weedless spoons are at home in matted milfoil or hydrilla, lily pads, duckweed, moss, logjams, etc.

Water temperature is a key factor in defining when the weedless spoon is most productive.

WHEN THE sun is high and the wind calm, fish will position themselves several feet into a line of lily pads or weeds.

Martin and Dance both agree on 70 degrees as a minimum surface temperature.

Martin says water temperature doesn't get too hot for spoon fishing. "Actually, when the water is really hot, bass move under matted vegetation, since the temperature under this cover is cooler. If you're wade fishing, which I like to do with spoons, you can feel the difference. The water under matted grass or lily pads will be noticeably cooler than in non-shaded water of the same depth."

Martin continues that other conditions determine how effective spoons will be on bass from one day to the next. "Usually, early morning and late afternoon are better times to fish spoons. Also, a cloudy day is far better than a bright, sunny one.

"If there's wind or current pushing in on a grassbed, shad may be washed up against the cover. If you see baitfish flipping along the outside edge of vegetation, that's an automatic spoon day.

"And water color can affect success with spoons," Martin adds. "Bass detect and strike this bait visually, so the water must at least be moderately clear so they can see it. Spoons aren't very effective in muddy water."

TACKLE FOR SPOONS

Dance and Martin employ brawny rods and thick line for fishing weedless spoons. Both anglers agree that such strength is warranted, considering the likelihood of battling trophy bass in the thickest possible cover.

"I use a 6- to 7-foot heavy-duty casting rod and reel," Dance informs. "The long rod has more sweep, which allows you to set the hook harder and put more pressure on fish in grass or brush. Also, I spool up with 30-pound-test (Stren) MagnaThin. I like this line's strength, small diameter and lack of stretch."

Martin uses a 7- to 7 1/2-foot heavy-action flipping rod and 20- to 30-pound-test Stren line. He notes, "I've had days on Okeechobee when anything less than 30-pound test was a mistake. You only sacrifice a little casting distance by using heavy line with this bait, and you have everything else to gain. I'd say 17-pound test would be the minimum size in any weedless spoon application."

METHODS FOR SPOONS

The two most common methods for fishing weedless spoons are sliding them over matted surface cover and swimming them just above the top of submerged vegetation. Bass hanging in this greenery notice a bait wobbling overhead and rush up and engulf it.

"Let's start out with a very important point," Martin urges. "Whenever you're fishing a weedless spoon, don't hold the rod sideways and pull it at an angle. Instead, always keep your rod pointed toward the bait. This allows you to manipulate it and nose it through cover without having it catch on grass or twigs and then skip forward. The idea is to keep the spoon running with a steady retrieve, not a jerky one. You want to make it as easy as possible for a fish to nail it, and a steady retrieve does this."

Another basic with spoons is to cast repeatedly to the same spot. Dance explains, "Say you're fishing in lily pads. When you cast in and reel your spoon back out, a bass down under the pads can hear the noise and see movement, but by the time he decides to investigate it, the spoon's gone. By making a second or third cast to the same spot, you give this fish time to find the bait and get excited. A lot of times a strike comes after that first cast."

Dance and Martin concentrate on working the outside edges of cover with weedless spoons.

"Rarely do you find many fish way back in the middle of large grassbeds or logjams," Martin advises. "Instead, they're usually close to the edges. So the best casting angles are those that cover as much edge as possible."

Sunlight and wind help position bass in weeds, he adds. "If the sun is high and the water is calm, bass will probably be a few feet back in the grass or moss," says Martin. "But if wind or current is pushing in on the cover, the fish will be closer to the edge. In this case I concentrate on points, holes and other likely features in the grass within a foot or two of open water."

Dance says a slow retrieve is preferable to a fast one. "I fish a spoon as slow as I can and still keep it on the surface," he says. "A slow presentation is more tantalizing. It gives the fish more time to decide to strike. Adding a Pork-O or a thick plastic trailer gives a spoon extra flotation and allows you to reduce your retrieve speed."

Coaxing bass to strike is only half the spoon fishing process. Hooking them is the other half.

"It's very common for a bass to blow up on a spoon and miss it entirely," Martin instructs. "Sometimes they'll hit two or three times on the same retrieve and never get it.

"If a fish blows up on your spoon and misses and then won't come back," Dance adds, "try this: Cast past where the strike occurred, reel the bait back up to the hole, then stop it and let it sink. More times than not, that bass will blast it. Then set the hook and pull the fish away from the cover before it has a chance to turn and burrow in."

In addition to fishing weedless spoons on the surface, Dance uses these lures with two underwater methods. The first applies to emergent grassbeds that top out beneath the surface.

"This is sort of like swimming a spinnerbait," he says. "You want the spoon to crawl just over the top of the grass. I do this with a pop-pop-pop action with my wrists. Or sometimes I may pop it a couple of times and reel it up to the surface. Then I'll let it settle back down, and repeat this process. You just have to vary your retrieve to see what the fish want."

Dance also works a black Timber King and pork eel slowly through timber, stumps and brush in relatively cold water. "You fish this bait like a worm, gliding it through the cover. It's a lot more fluid than a jig. This is a good presentation when bass are first moving up shallow after winter," he explains.

The Art Of Spooning

The pros recommend a long, medium-heavy baitcasting rod and heavy mono or braided line for weedless spoons. The long rod facilitates longer casts and helps power a big bass out of thick grass.

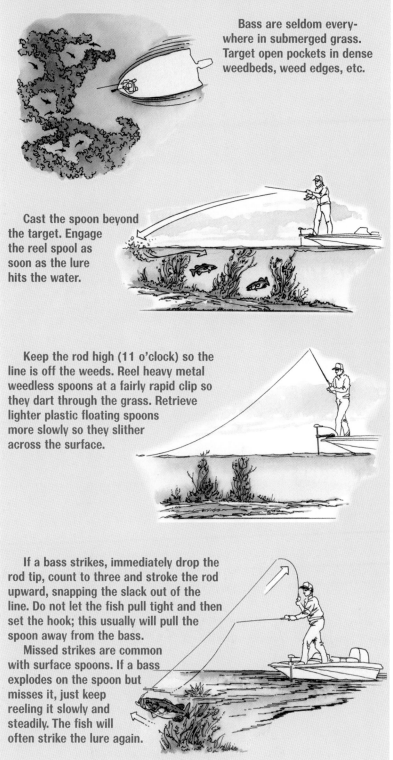

Bass are seldom everywhere in submerged grass. Target open pockets in dense weedbeds, weed edges, etc.

Cast the spoon beyond the target. Engage the reel spool as soon as the lure hits the water.

Keep the rod high (11 o'clock) so the line is off the weeds. Reel heavy metal weedless spoons at a fairly rapid clip so they dart through the grass. Retrieve lighter plastic floating spoons more slowly so they slither across the surface.

If a bass strikes, immediately drop the rod tip, count to three and stroke the rod upward, snapping the slack out of the line. Do not let the fish pull tight and then set the hook; this usually will pull the spoon away from the bass.

Missed strikes are common with surface spoons. If a bass explodes on the spoon but misses it, just keep reeling it slowly and steadily. The fish will often strike the lure again.

THE BUZZBAIT draws both hunger and reflex strikes.

NOT JUST A NOISEMAKER

Decades of experience with these buzzing topwaters has taught the pros important lessons

RICK CLUNN STILL CRINGES when his partner ties one on. Larry Lazoen says he fishes one at least 50 percent of the time in Florida. And Jim Morton believes the lure sees some use in nearly every tournament, except those in extremely cold weather. Jimmy Crisp even uses one in cold water, and he catches 5-pound smallmouth with it.

Which lure are these well-known anglers describing? The buzzbait — possibly the most misunderstood lure in bass fishing today. While buzzbaits do not win many national tournaments outright, they play a significant role in many of them. And they certainly deserve a place in any recreational fisherman's tacklebox.

"Most anglers have a lot of preconceived ideas about buzzbaits," says Crisp, a Tennessee lure designer and former tournament pro. "They think buzzbaits can only be used under limited conditions, such as early and late during the day around shallow heavy cover or when the water temperature is warm.

"The correct water temperature for buzzbaits is probably the biggest misconception. I was one of the believers in the warmwater theory," he admits. "Then, one December day I went out on Lake Cherokee to tune some buzzbaits for an upcoming Florida trip. My first cast to a rock-and-mud flat was nailed by a 5-pound smallmouth."

Morton, director of promotions for Rapala, has had plenty of experience fishing buzzbaits in cold water.

(Opposite page) RICK CLUNN defies conventional buzzbait logic by fishing the lure when most anglers think the water is still too cold. When the water reaches 50 degrees, he begins using the lure.

Topwater Tips

No law says you have to use a white or chartreuse buzzbait. In fact, it's one of the pros' closely held secrets that black buzzbaits can be even more effective than white ones, especially in heavily pressured water. Try a black buzzer over weedbeds, around brushpiles and adjacent to laydowns. They might also have an edge over lighter-colored baits in low light conditions, such as overcast days and dawn and dusk. A great technique when fishing ponds where bass prowl the edges is to throw a black buzzbait onto the shore (cover permitting) and drag it into the water. Begin retrieving as soon as the bait leaves dry land. Where you can't cast onto the bank, aim for the water's edge. A couple of feet too short, and you'll miss an explosive strike.

He credits a buzzbait for a win on Oklahoma's Grand Lake.

"As long as you have fairly shallow, active bass, a buzzbait will draw strikes," says Morton, who also tried a regular topwater plug during that tournament, but without results.

"The water temperature had dropped steadily into the mid-50s, but the bass were still shallow. They never stopped hitting a buzzbait, even in the wind and rain, and under severe cold-front conditions."

"There definitely are prime times to fish a buzzbait," adds Clunn. "I try to be the first to fish it in late winter/early spring. Some of the biggest bass you'll catch on a buzzbait are when most anglers think the water is still too cold. I like the temperature to be in the mid-50s and rising.

"From then on, the lure will produce well throughout the spring. My next favorite time is in the fall, when the temperature is 65 degrees and dropping and you can find shallow, active fish."

He also fishes a buzzbait in summer, but he reserves it for traditional topwater times: early and late in the day.

Clunn is the angler most responsible for introducing buzzbaits to mainstream bass fishing. His 1977 BASS Champs win on Tennessee's Percy Priest Lake was the first time many of the pros had ever seen a buzzbait. Later that year, Clunn won the Bassmaster Classic title in which a buzzbait also played a major role.

"The appeal of the buzzbait to bass is difficult to understand," he says. "The only real reason I can think of why bass hit the lure is because they're aggressive — the lure immediately gets their attention.

"After that, there could be multiple reasons a bass strikes, including reflexes. Bass could even be playing with the lure. I honestly think, after watching the bass in my pond chase dragonflies, that sometimes the fish will just play with a lure the way a cat will sometimes play with a mouse."

BUZZBAITS WILL produce over submerged cover in open water.

Lazoen of Port Charlotte, Fla., agrees in part, adding, "I believe bass hit lures for just three reasons: out of hunger, out of defense and as a pure reflex. A buzzbait draws both hunger and reflex strikes, which makes it a pretty important lure for anyone to use."

One of the major reasons buzzbaits do not get heavier use among the pros, he says, is because any topwater bite is usually fairly fragile; that is, it is easily disrupted by changing conditions like wind, water clarity, barometric pressure, fishing pressure and changes in water temperature.

"All these affect a fish's willingness to come to the surface," points out Clunn. "To me, buzzbaits are basically shallow to middepth lures, although I have brought bass to the surface from 20 to 30 feet in clear water."

Clunn likes to fish buzzbaits in murky water, in contrast to the many anglers who feel the lure is best suited to clear conditions.

"Murky water helps keep bass shallow," says the four time world champion. "Unlike other topwater lures that rely more on visual attraction, a buzzbait works because of the disturbance it creates. That's what brings bass out to investigate."

Another misconception anglers have is that the buzzbait always has to be fished around cover. Not so, says Crisp.

"A buzzbait definitely works best around cover," he explains, "but you can fish a buzzbait in open water, especially over underwater structure. In Lake Cherokee, there isn't much cover, but there is plenty of structure. The joy of using a buzzbait is that it pulls bass out of both cover and structure to hit.

"You don't have to present the lure directly to the fish. I think the only other lure that may also do this is a fast moving spinnerbait."

When he's fishing murky water, Clunn works the lure as slow as he can reel it and still keep it on top. If he's fishing targets, he casts beyond that target, reels quickly to it, then slows the retrieve and lets the buzzbait hit the target. By moving his rod angle, he guides the lure around the side and even the front of the target.

In clear water, the best retrieve is a fast one, he says. He also uses a smaller buzzbait, as well as some of the new transparent skirts.

Clunn's favorite skirt colors are white and chartreuse in murky water, transparent skirts in clear water and black skirts on really dark, overcast days.

One of the major complaints anglers have always had with buzzbaits has been missed strikes. Morton believes one of the reasons may be that bass are striking the commotion-causing blades rather than the skirt.

"In the tournament I won on Grand Lake, the buzzbait I used had a bent-head shaft," he notes. "That caused the head, skirt and hook to ride lower in the water. I

Going In-line Buzzing

An in-line buzzer not only produced several big fish for Roland Martin early in his career, but it was his secret weapon in a couple of national tournament wins.

"When you want a weedless buzzbait with a more quiet presentation," says Martin, "you can't beat it."

The in-line buzzer — be it Floyd's or Uncle Buck's — shouldn't be considered as a replacement for the more popular, safety-pin-style buzzbaits that make more noise and can be fished slightly slower.

"My buzzbait is merely a tool," insists Pat Floyd, designer and maker of the Floyd's Buzzer. "It's got a different sound than the overhead buzzbaits and can be fished through surface vegetation where other buzzbaits that sit lower in the water can't be fished."

Martin agrees. Because it produces a softer surface noise and is more weedless, he says its ideal for when bass are a little spooky.

"Everybody thinks you need a loud buzzbait, but there are times when quieter buzzbaits like the Buzzer are better," he explains. "A good example is when the pollen is on the water and bass are spawning around flooded willow brush in calm pockets. That subtle 'patter-patter-patter' sound gets the bass' attention without spooking them."

BUZZBAITS AS SEARCH BAITS

Buzzers will show you the biggest, most aggressive bass in the area

THE ONE THING LOST in most discussions about buzzbaits is the topic of finding fish. Too often, bass anglers focus on the big fish capabilities of these lures and not on their use as pure search baits.

To be sure, someone like Texan Dean Rojas appreciates the quality strikes buzzbaits can produce.

But he also recognizes that buzzbaits — used properly — can tell him precisely where to fish.

"Anytime from late spring to late fall, the buzzbait becomes an excellent search bait, one that can cover an incredible amount of water in a relatively short time," notes Rojas.

"If I'm practicing for a tournament, I just want

them to hit it. My goal is simply to locate the fish. In fact, many times I'll cover my hooks."

According to Rojas, his buzzbait search offers three distinct advantages: First, bass that respond to the water-churning presentation of a buzzbait are generally the most aggressive in a given area. And typically, these also are some of the largest fish. From the most basic perspective, this tells him that a certain zone does hold quality fish and should be factored in as part of his tournament game plan. But it does much more than that.

"What these strikes are really telling me is that a lot more is going on than just what I'm seeing," he says. "It tells me that the zone I've discovered has the necessary ingredients for quality fish, and there is a good chance it holds more than one bass. In most cases, if you can get a strike on a buzzbait, usually there are two or three more around that will eat a crank or a spinnerbait."

The second advantage for Rojas is in being able to see the quality of fish that are responding to his lure, something vitally important during a pretournament practice period. And finally, he places great stock in the buzzbait's ability to rapidly cover water while still providing information about the bass population below.

In describing the ideal situation for buzzbait action, Rojas would opt for a midsummer scenario with 85 to 90 degree water temperatures and air temps in the high 80s. The skies would offer cloudy, overcast conditions — perhaps with thunderstorms cycling through — to offer the kind of low light periods otherwise available only early or late in the day.

"You have to judge what the fish want. Although low light conditions offer the best condi-

tions, I've had bass eat buzzbaits under a high sun," counsels Rojas.

"Too often, I think many fishermen feel as though they need perfect conditions to even tie on a buzzbait. What they must realize is that buzzbaits can be discouraging because they're not especially high percentage lures when it comes to hooking and landing fish. They would rather throw something like a spinnerbait with a more dependable strike-to-hookup ratio."

Of course, the difference in approach is that Rojas wants to find the fish first. If they're aggressive enough to eat the buzzbait, the Arizona pro starts his day with some kicker fish in the livewell. Then, armed with the confidence of having turned fish up in several areas, he can buckle down, using any number of higher percentage baits to fill out his limit.

The Trailer Debate

Adding a plastic trailer to a buzzbait is said to give the bait added strike appeal. What is more, adding a trailer hook to this bladed contraption is said to increase the odds of a hook set.

Ohio pro Joe Thomas disagrees with the first theory and agrees with the other. Here's why.

"I just don't use plastic trailers because they increase the odds of missed strikes," he says. "The fish is already striking the bait as it churns across the surface. The added bulk of the plastic can cause it to get waded up over the hook point, causing you to lose a fish."

On the other hand, he does advocate the use of a trailer hook on a buzzbait in open water or sparse cover, where there is little chance of snagging.

"I don't like a trailer hook that's fixed. Instead, I want one that swings freely on the shank of the main hook. It's held in place by a plastic tab between it and the barb of the main hook."

Topwater Tips

■ **Description** — A single-blade, 1/2-ounce buzzbait.
■ **Colors** — Depends on water clarity. In stained water, gold, copper or black blades with white, chartreuse or black skirts. In clear water, silver blades with translucent, shad-pattern skirts.
■ **Rod** — 7-foot Browning (medium).
■ **Reel** — Quantum E600Ti (6.3:1 gear ratio).
■ **Line** — 17-pound or heavier Berkley Big Game (clear).
■ **Alterations** — Rojas bends down the head slightly to make the bait run lower in the water. Also, he adds a No. 4 treble hook (held in place with aquarium tubing fitted over the eye of the treble) as a stinger. "You don't get hung up as much as you might imagine — plus it's saved my bacon on short strikes many times."

SOFT SURFACE LURES

Rats, frogs and snakes:

Creeping critters that bass love to hate . . .

TOPWATER WORMS

From bare banks to thick cover, these wild-colored worms are amazingly versatile bass fishing tools

THIS MUST BE THE PLACE where the phrase "bare bank" was first coined. On this brisk spring day, Ken Cook slows his boat as he approaches a stretch of shoreline that lies between some of the best looking, cover laden banks in all of Bull Shoals Reservoir. Cook then kicks his trolling motor on high and powers away from the picturesque portion of the shore.

All that lies ahead is a long, shallow flat with nothing resembling bass cover, except for pea-size gravel.

Reaching into his rod box, the former Bassmaster Classic champion abandons his earlier game plan and removes a rod sporting a bright orange Berkley Power Floating Worm. "This kind of bank is perfect for a floating worm," he says, in part out of confidence and in part, apparently, seeking confirmation of his theory. "It's the kind of bank that people will overlook, and a floating worm will find the fish if they're here."

Surprisingly, it doesn't take long for the floating worm to work its magic. Individual bass suddenly appear from out of nowhere, rising stealthily to the surface to gently mouth the neon worm. By the time he has covered the 50-yard stretch of bank, Cook will have collected a nice limit of largemouth — far better than he had done fishing the "textbook" areas dotted with boat docks, trees and logs.

It was another demonstration of the allure of the floating worm, which remains one of the most underrated and underutilized of all bass lures.

"People put too many limitations on floating worms," believes Davy Hite, another former BASS world-titleholder, from Prosperity, S.C. "They limit themselves by only fishing it during certain times of the year or during certain situations. They get too specific with the lure.

(Opposite page)
THE POSTSPAWN is the absolute prime time for fishing with floating worms.

Topwater Tips

Especially when they first came into wide use, most floating worms were poured in bright colors: bubblegum, chartreuse, banana, white and merthiolate. The fish didn't seem to be turned off by the wild hues, and fishermen loved being able to see their worms as they twitched them just under the surface. When the worm disappears, set the hook, some anglers recommended. But bass in heavily fished waters have begun to shy away from brightly colored floating worms. If that's the case where you fish, switch to earth tones and traditional dark worm colors, like junebug, pumpkinseed and watermelon. You'll get more strikes, even if you can't see them happen.

THE PROS HAVE UNCOVERED other applications for soft jerkbaits besides fishing them in heavy cover.

GOING SOFT WITH JERKBAITS

For more versatility and bigger bass, try one of these potbelly twitch baits

I T STANDS TO REASON that angler applications of soft jerkbaits have expanded beyond their original function as a weightless, shallow water bass seducer.

After all, it has been more than a decade since Lunker City lit up the bass fishing world with the Slug-Go, the forerunner to dozens of other soft plastic jerkbait shapes and designs that have emerged in recent years. And as manufacturers broaden the soft plastic jerkbait category, anglers devise new ways to fish them.

Despite the subtle differences in the myriad choices, all of these slender slices of soft plastic have a deep groove in their bulging bellies to help hide a single hook when rigged Texas style. With the barb skin-hooked and lying along the top side of the lure, the notched belly reduces the amount of plastic along the shank that can interfere with the hook set.

(Opposite page) RECOGNIZING THAT schooling fish have voracious appetites, Ray Sedgwick rigs soft jerkbaits in tandem to double the chances of a hookup.

"Methods for fishing these baits are limited only by one's imagination," says Craig Daniel, an Alabama pro and soft jerkbait expert.

For example, Daniel likes to swim potbellied Zoom Flukes over shallow vegetation in Florida; he twitches them adjacent to steep bluffs in deep, clear lakes; he flips them into heavy cover; he fishes them on Carolina rigs in deep water; and he even uses them as spinnerbait trailers for slow rolling the bottom.

And when it comes to traditional shallow water twitch bait fishing, Arizona pro Mark Kile says the lure's unique sinking action sets it apart from other soft jerkbaits.

"A lot of baits look great in the water as you twitch them along, but when you stop the bait, it rocks gently from side to side as it falls," explains Kile. "The subtle rocking

Topwater Tips

After the Slug-Go craze began to die down, soft jerkbaits morphed from slugs into shad look-alikes. These potbelly jerkbaits are especially versatile — great for spawning and postspawn bass, for schooling fish and for fall fishing when shad move into the backs of creeks. You'll need wide gap hooks for these babies. A 4/0 wide gap will fit most models nicely. Be sure to "Tex-pose" the hooks by running the barb all the way through the body and rigging it so the barb lays flat on the lure's back. You can make it even more weedless by slipping the tip of the barb just under the skin of the lure.

SOFT FLOATING STICKS FOR BASS

You couldn't design a bass lure that looks more lifeless than a stickworm — until it hits the water

EVERY DECADE OR SO, A SOFT PLASTIC BAIT comes along that revolutionizes the way we fish for bass. First, there was Creme's original Scoundrel worm, followed by the phenomenon of the Texas rig. Bobby Garland's Gitzit later launched the tube boom. Just when major innovations seemed hopelessly dormant, Lunker City's Slug-Go started the soft plastic stickbait craze. And now we have Yamamoto's Senko.

Of all these lures, the banal Senko wins the prize for being the most unlikely sensation. This pudgy, blunt-nose cylinder, adorned with shallow rings and a slightly tapered tail, sprouts no wings, no skirts and no undulating appendages to impart action. It doesn't closely resemble anything bass eat; it looks like a poor crawler imitation at best. All it does is catch the fire out of bass.

Lure maker Gary Yamamoto, a regular on the CITGO Bassmaster Tour, claims the Slug-Go gave him the inspiration to invent the Senko.

"I saw the need for a plastic bait that would cast a long way like the Slug-Go, but would have a different kind of action," says Yamamoto. "I loaded the plastic with salt to increase its casting weight and to make it sink faster."

During the design phase, Yamamoto focused on a lure that would deliver a gliding, darting action when retrieved as a twitch bait. He was pleased when his brainchild lived up to his expectations in this department. However, he didn't envision the lure's horizontal posture when allowed to sink without a weight, or its subtle side-to-side tail-wagging motion as

(Opposite page) ALLOWING A Senko to free-fall next to shallow cover will coax quality strikes, according to inventor Gary Yamamoto.

Topwater Tips

The problem with Senkos and similar "stickworms" is that they tear up so easily. The supersoft plastic is important in attracting strikes and coaxing bass to hold on to the lures, but it also means that you'll have to put on a new bait after every two or three strikes. Fortunately, you can hook these lures through either end. When the larger, blunt end tears up, rig through the pointed "tail" section. And after both ends are battered, hook them through the middle, wacky style. All three setups are deadly, and in most situations, one works as well as the other.

it falls. These unintended qualities have made the Senko one of the most effective finesse baits of all time.

"Sometimes you get lucky," says Yamamoto. "All you have to do is cast the Senko next to cover and let it sink on a semislack line. The bass swim out to take it. I fish it that way as deep as 10 feet. It also works great on bedded bass."

This is exactly how Yamamoto fished a 5-inch Senko at a recent Tour event at Lake Guntersville, Ala. He coaxed many strikes by letting the bait waggle down next to shallow cover, such as stumps, rock ledges and aquatic vegetation. When the bait touched down, he hopped it up and let it sink again. The slow, subdued action was more than the bass could stand. Yamamoto also duped a number of spawning bass by letting the Senko free-fall into their beds.

By the end of the tournament, Yamamoto had culled four limits of bass that totaled 70 pounds. It was good enough for sixth place and important points that helped him earn a berth to the 2002 Bassmaster Classic.

Of the six sizes of Senkos now available, from 2 to 7 inches, Yamamoto favors the 5-inch model. He generally fares better with all sizes in clear water, where bass can see the baits easily and be induced by their titillating action. Watermelon, pumpkin and laminated watermelon-pumpkin are his most productive clear water colors. In murky water, he switches to black and other dark colors.

When he casts to fairly open targets, Yamamoto rigs the Senko with a 3/0 Gamakatsu EWG offset hook. Thick cover dictates a 5/0 Gamakatsu EWG straight-shank hook, especially when he resorts to flippin' and pitchin' presentations. If he needs a faster sink rate to spark reflex strikes, Yamamoto adds a 1/8- or 3/16-ounce Gambler Florida Rig screw-lock bullet sinker. The sinker also helps the bait penetrate dense cover.

"With a weight, the Senko drops with a gliding action," says Yamamoto. "And it has a tendency to spin to the right or left. Bass respond aggressively toward it."

Yamamoto fishes the Senko on a 7-foot Mod III medium action baitcasting rod made by his own company. It features a Loomis blank. He matches the rod with 14- or 16-pound-test fluorocarbon Sugoi Clear Line, which he claims sinks well, is strong and abrasion resistant.

Of course, Yamamoto isn't the only angler catching bass with the Senko. It has been one of the hottest baits on professional tournament circuits over the past two seasons. In response, other lure manufacturers have introduced a number of Senko clones.

Bass Pro Shops offers the Stick-O and Stick-O-Lite. The latter model is more buoyant and falls so slowly it nearly suspends. Zoom's fat 5 1/2-inch Z-Nail has pronounced body segments. Alton Jones relied on the Yum Dinger to win the 2003 California Showdown, a CITGO Tour event at Clear Lake.

Also, don't overlook Pure Fishing's Gulp Sinking Minnow, the Flash from Kinami Baits, Luck 'E' Strike's Jogger Worm, Chomper's Salty Sinker, and the Tiki-Stick and Bamboo-Stick from Wave

Worms. The Bamboo-Stick is a rotund bait that has big bass appeal.

Texan Dean Rojas, who claimed instant fame by setting the all-time catch records at Florida's Lake Toho, dotes on Lake Fork Trophy Bait & Tackle's 4-inch Ring Fry and Hawg Caller's 5-inch Teezo Worm. He rigs both baits with a heavy 5/0 offset worm hook to give them additional casting weight, increase the sink rate and improve hook sets. He rigs the hook Tex-posed and skin hooks the point.

"Both baits have thick bodies and lots of salt," says Rojas. "The lighter Ring Fry has deep rings that release air bubbles and give it a softer feel. I fish it a lot around grass and rocks. The Teezo is bigger and sinks faster. I like to throw it around stuff like flooded brush and wood cover."

Rojas fishes both baits with a 6-foot, 6-inch, medium-heavy Quantum baitcasting rod. He goes with 12-pound mono when casting the Ring Fry, and 17-pound with the Teezo. He credits the Ring Fry for a 10th place finish on the California Delta that clinched the 1999-2000 Angler-of-the-Year title in the Western Open Division. He was casting the red bug color without a weight to hydrilla and riprap in depths from 1 to 6 feet. He believes many of the bass he caught were on beds, but he couldn't see them due to limited water visibility.

"I've caught bass on these baits in everything from clear water to chocolate mud," says Rojas. "In dirty water, I fish red bug or junebug. I like watermelon-fire in clear water."

Rojas generally fishes the Ring Fry and Teezo no deeper than 6 feet, though he does let them sink as deep as 15 feet in ultraclear Western reservoirs, such as Lake Mead. In clear water, he sometimes pulls bass up from deeper water, including suspended fish. He employs these baits mainly during the prespawn, spawn and postspawn periods, but also has done well with them in the fall. Regardless of the season, he encourages bites with a deadstick routine.

"I cast next to cover, hold my rod tip at about 10 o'clock and fish the bow in my line," says Rojas. "When the bait touches bottom, I keep the

Fries As Senkos

Given the success of the falling Senko presentation, some anglers have begun fishing fry worms in a similar fashion. Mark Menendez, a regular on the CITGO Tour, does so with a 4-inch Riverside Rib Fry. He also fares well working the Rib Fry as a finesse stickbait with a jerk-jerk, pause; jerk-jerk, pause cadence.

While Menendez believes most anglers will be more proficient using spinning tackle to cast the light Rib Fry, he manages nicely with a 6-foot, 6-inch medium-heavy Pflueger baitcasting rod, and a Pflueger Trion reel filled with 8- or 10-pound Excalibur line.

When rigging the Rib Fry Texas style, Menendez uses a 3/0 offset worm hook. He switches to a straight-shank 3/0 worm hook when he rigs the bait wacky style.

"I go with the wacky rig a lot when I'm after spawning bass," says Menendez. "I keep the boat moving through an area and fan cast the bait while I concentrate on looking for beds. By holding the rod low and working the bait with a rhythm, I can set the hook the moment I feel any kind of resistance. Many times, I'll catch a big female doing this."

Should Menendez spot a bass on a bed, he'll toss the wacky Rib Fry to the fish to see how it responds. In many instances, one cast is all it takes. If the bass shows an interest in the Rib Fry, he sticks with it on subsequent casts.

Docks, stumps, laydowns and other hard cover prompt Menendez to go with a Texas rig, a 5/0 offset hook, and 20-pound line to extract bass from the abrasive cover. He usually flips and pitches the bait and lets it slowly penetrate the cover without a weight.

"That's not something you want to do when the wind blows," says Menendez. "But when conditions are right, the Rib Fry catches bass better than weighted worms and jigs."

rod still and crank two or three times on the reel and let it sink again. It's a real soft presentation."

When starting out the day, Rojas fishes the Ring Fry and Teezo most of the way back to the boat to see if bass are loosely related to cover, or following the bait before they strike. If he determines that the bites are occurring close to cover, he cranks in after two or three drops.

"I never use these baits to search for bass," says Rojas. "They're too slow. I find bass with crankbaits, spinnerbaits or other lures that cover water faster. I deadstick fries only when I know where bass are located, and usually after they quit biting other baits."

FAKE FROGS are effective search lures in dense surface growth because they can be fished quickly and cover a broad range of territory.

FROGS, RATS AND POPPERS

Bass have no place to hide when these lures are used to dig them out of even the thickest weed cover

I N HOT WEATHER, WHEN LILY PADS, milfoil, hydrilla, hyacinths and pond scum form dense mats across the water, few lures are as effective — or more fun to fish — as soft plastic frogs, rats and poppers. These weedless artificials, often called "scum baits," are known for catching big bass in the toughest places to fish and are often used by BASS pros in weedy situations.

MEET THE FAMILY

There are several varieties of soft plastic "scum baits" on the market:

• *Frogs* — These were the original soft plastic weedless lures. They are very effective when fished across all types of surface cover, and work especially well over lily pads in shallow, natural lakes and ponds.

(Opposite page) FROGS ARE a natural food source for bass where both creatures coexist in the swampy habitat indigenous to lily pads.

• *Rats* — These cylindrical lures look like mice and usually have some sort of appendage or tail at the end. They were developed primarily for fishing surface algae and milfoil mats, but work well in any matted, surface weed situation.

• *Poppers* — These soft plastic baits have a scooped-out face and can emit a loud popping sound when the rod tip is jerked. They produce best when at least a couple of inches of water covers dense weed growth.

TACKLE FOR THE FAMILY

Casting these baits can be a problem. The dense weed growth for which they are intended demands stout baitcasting gear. But unlike heavy flipping jigs or

Topwater Tips

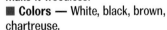

■ **Description** — A 1/2-ounce, hollow-bodied plastic frog equipped with two upturned hooks with points that lie close to the body to make it weedless.

■ **Colors** — White, black, brown, chartreuse.

■ **Bait alterations** — Sharpen hooks to long, tapered, conical points. Don't add extra weight when walking frogs. Remove approximately one-third of the leg skirt material by cutting with scissors (pulling out the strands can loosen the entire bundle). Use a black marker to add spots to the lure belly for a more natural appearance.

■ **Rod** — 6 1/2-foot Competitive Edge worm/jig rod (medium heavy).

■ **Line** — 50-pound Berkley Whiplash braided line.

area of surface weed cover faster than might be possible with other types of weedless lures.

Bassmaster Classic qualifier Joe Thomas has fished these baits for years, and recommends these places to try them:

• *Holes, pockets and edges* — "Lily pads, matted junk weeds and surface scum all hold lots of big bass, but concentrations of fish tend to gather at the edges of the bed, in small indentations or pockets along the outer perimeter of the bed and close to open holes within the vegetation."

• *Where surface vegetation meets a shallow shoreline* — "Here, the pads, junk weeds or scum covering the water act as an extension of the shore itself. Terrestrial creatures, such as snakes, frogs, small mammals, even birds, have no problem moving from the bank across these thick surface weeds; bass locate at this edge to take advantage of these feeding opportunities. This pattern is typically most productive early and late in the day."

• *Far back in dense surface weeds, where a boat can't go* — "Use them where the surface covering is so thick your boat simply can't get back into a spot, or you don't want to risk spooking bass by churning your way through the pads or grass with your trolling motor. Making long casts with frogs and rats is a good way to cover this seemingly unreachable water."

• *Where surface growth intersects some other structural element* — "A good spot is where a ditch or small channel winding through a shallow flat is covered with pads, junk weeds or scum. You may notice a slight change in the density of the surface cover where this occurs. Any secondary structural element will help concentrate bass in a weedy lake."

• *Where two or more types of weed growth occur in the same area* — "Often, more than one type of surface weed is found in the same body of water. Places where they come together will often draw in major concentrations of bass."

spinnerbaits, soft plastic weedless lures are very light in weight, making them difficult to cast on many types of heavy tackle.

Most pros prefer long, medium-heavy action rods for fishing these weedless wonders. Rods 7 to 7 1/2 feet are recommended; these should have some give to the tip. Instead of a graphite rod, which may be overly stiff, try a fiberglass or composite rod, which can "load up" more easily with a light lure and allows the bass time to mouth the bait when it strikes. Use a baitcasting reel and heavy mono (20- to 30-pound test) or braided line.

FISHING THE SLOP

Bass are seldom everywhere in weedy lakes. But soft plastic weedless baits are effective "search" lures in dense surface growth. They can be fished fairly quickly and allow an angler to cover a broad

ADD A STINGER hook to weedless rats and frogs when the fish are striking short.

CHUCKING AND WINDING

Using a long, powerful baitcasting rod, cast the lure well past holes or edges that can concentrate fish. Hold the rod at 11 o'clock so the line stays well off the surface of the weeds. Reel the lure fairly slowly so it crawls and tumbles across the surface weeds.

If a bass explodes on the lure, immediately lower the rod tip to 9 o'clock. If the line doesn't go tight, don't set the hook — the fish doesn't have the lure. Return the rod to 11 o'clock and continue the retrieve. However, if the line moves, count to three and set the hook hard with a solid upward stroke of the rod.

Add A Stinger To Your Frog

Some anglers feel that adding legs to these lures adds an enticing action, particularly around thinner cover. Others also feel that adding a stinger hook on top of the lure reduces the number of missed fish. Here's how it's done with a Frog from Mann's Bait Co.

1) Remove the hook assembly by pushing the Frog forward over the eye of the hook.

2) With pliers, remove the eyelet from the hook assembly.

3) Rotate the eyelet over 180 degrees and reattach. This is necessary for the following steps to work.

4) Bend the eyelet eye up 90 degrees. Open it, slip on a No. 1 Eagle Claw bait hook. The 90 degree bend allows the bait hook to lie flat against the eyelet assembly.

5) Thread your fishing line through the Frog body and tie to the eyelet. This is to help guide the hook assembly through the lure.

6) Pull the hook assembly into the Frog so the eyelet is in place at the head of the lure. Use your fingers to feel the stinger hook through the frog. Punch the barb through the top of the Frog between the eyes.

To add legs, remove the Frog's skirt while the hook assembly is out of the lure body (Step 2). Thread on curl-tail grubs after Step 6.

To add a stinger hook, push body forward and remove hook assembly.

Remove and open eyelet, then attach stinger hook to front eye.

Close the eyelet, tie on line, and thread assembly back through Frog.

A modified rat lure remains weedless because the hooks point up.

Once it's certain the fish has been hooked, keep the rod high and reel very quickly, moving the bass to the top of the grass as fast as possible. Then skate the fish over the top of the vegetation into open water where it can be landed safely. If the fish can't be brought to the surface before it tangles in dense weeds, try to go to the fish to free it rather than pulling too hard. Otherwise, the hooks might be ripped from its mouth.

TINKERING AROUND

These lures are inexpensive and relatively easy to modify, so many anglers experiment with ways to make them work better. Here are some suggestions:

A soft plastic rat or frog can be made more "castable," without compromising its flotation, by cutting a slit in the back with a sharp knife and stuffing small pieces of plastic worm inside. Adding a few glass worm rattles will make the lure noisier and make it easier for bass to locate it in dense surface growth.

For greater action and attraction, cut the legs off a soft plastic frog and run two spinnerbait skirts through the twin hooks so the skirts dangle out the back.

Poke a small hole in the back of one of these lures and fill the hollow body cavity with liquid fish attractant. The scent will leach out as the lure crawls across the surface grass.

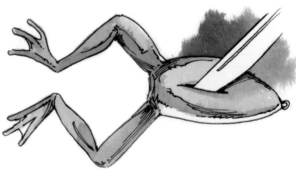

Punch a hole in the bottom of a rubber frog so it will fill with water and sink slowly. This slow-sinking presentation is deadly when bass are holding beneath the edges of lily pads and surface scum and refuse to strike a lure on the surface. It also works well for bedding bass in open water. When the lure has filled completely with water, squeeze the water out and recast.

If the frog or rat snags on lily pads or hyacinths, bend the hooks slightly inward with pliers.

PICK A COLOR

Many pros favor bright colors for these lures, believing that bass need all the help they can get to locate them in thick surface cover. White, bubble-gum pink, chartreuse, yellow and hot orange work well.

Frog Hopping Out West

With 1,000 miles of California Delta waterway to fish — as well as the tule-laden shore of Clear Lake — top western pro Mark Rizk has become very, very good at fishing artificial frogs.

Even so, Rizk has not fallen in love with the thick, matted cover that so many anglers associate with frog fishing. Yes, floating mats and tangled cover do offer some of the most predictable — and productive — outlets for these frogs and rats, and similar weedless plastics. But too often, he says, fishermen limit themselves to working these lures in places where no other baits will go.

"The fish aren't always under the thick mats. I'll look for them in areas with sparse weeds around other types of structure, such as docks, riprap banks and current breaks," remarks the 37-year-old pro.

"I consider a frog to be a weedless Zara Spook that can be thrown just about anywhere."

By expanding the places where he'll use the bait, Rizk has opened up the frog calendar to nearly a year-round proposition. In California, only December and January are frogless months, notes Rizk, who believes that any angler, anywhere, can and should use them more often.

In addition to the multitude of target areas available in summer, Rizk looks for weed die-offs in the fall, places where small weed clumps or sparse weedbeds concentrate fish forced out of expansive grassbeds as they died back. Once this vegetation starts growing around prespawn and spawning zones again in spring (and once water tem-

peratures hit the 60 degree mark), the frog again starts drawing strikes.

Whether Rizk is fishing tidal water around current edges or a reservoir situation with docks, the key to productive sparse cover is the structure elements nearby.

"The more types of desirable structure I can find in one area, the better chance I have of finding fish there. So, if you've got some docks that normally hold fish — with a few sparse weeds around them — it's almost a guarantee of success."

However, using frogs in areas where Zara Spooks can't go is just one part of the equation. Learning to fish them like this legendary stickbait is what really makes the difference.

"It takes more of a subtle touch than a Zara Spook. It's a matter of leaving a little slack in your line, so you're popping that slack with your rod tip. Slow down on your reel handle a bit and leave some slack in your line. Popping that slack is what gets the frog to walk."

Unfortunately, many fisher-

men accustomed to working frogs over heavy mats make the mistake of using the same stout tackle when trying to walk frogs in open water. Scaling down is part of the program, notes Rizk, who recommends a 6 1/2-foot medium heavy worm-and-jig rod spooled with a limber, no-stretch 50-pound braid like Berkley Whiplash.

If the water clarity offers a foot or more of visibility, Rizk is confident his frog-walking approach will work. He is especially certain of the enhanced strike-to-hookup ratio generated in open water conditions. Should a bass actually miss the bait, the Californian will stop it for a few seconds to make the bass think it has injured the frog. If there is no response within 15 seconds, he'll resume the walk. If these bait "kisses" continue, Rizk will then resort to a follow-up lure, such as a worm, jig or Slug-Go.

"Even if bass are not eating the frog, it is still a great fish locator. As long as you can get them to come up and look, it tells you a good fish is there."

SEASONAL SURFACE SITUATIONS

Think topwaters are only good
in hot weather? Guess again . . .

TOPWATER TIME IN THE NORTH

In Northern waters, especially those in the Midwest, summer is one long surface fishing season

I F YOU'RE ONE OF THOSE NORTHERN ANGLERS who limit topwater fishing to early morning and late evening periods, you're making a big mistake.

Those certainly are the prime periods for fast topwater action. But as some veteran Northern bass fishermen know, Northern lake conditions often are ideal for good surface explosions from sunup to sundown.

"I will have one tied to a rod, and it will be used sometime during the day, no matter what," says Michigan angler Mark Zona. "You should never discount a surface bait as a potential bass catcher on these waters."

Especially in clear water lakes, where a tantalizing topwater can draw bass from long distances; or the Great Lakes, where water temperatures hold bass relatively shallow all summer long; and smallmouth lakes, where brown fish aren't bashful about busting a lure walked over the top any time of day.

Topwaters stay effective longer for a number of reasons. The typically cooler water of Northern lakes helps hold bass shallower, and clearer water makes surface lures more visible to fish living at a variety of depths. Furthermore, abundant vegetation on most Northern lakes is ideally suited for working lures overhead.

Are there bad times? Sure. But on most Northern glacial lakes, universally accepted rules that were written for Southern reservoir fishing don't always apply.

"You just have to let the fish tell you when the time is right," adds Zona. "About the only mistake you can

(Opposite page) KEVIN VANDAM likes chuggers in heavy cover because they send out a deep "blooping" sound.

Topwater Tips

Most fishermen know to match the size, shape and color of a lure to the baitfish they're after. More advanced anglers also select lures according to the seasonal and weather patterns under which they're fishing. For example, the bigger, heavier Zara Spook gets the nod in murky water and when bass aren't exactly in a mood to chase a fast moving lure. But in clear water, you often have to keep a walking or darting bait moving, so the fish doesn't get a good look at it. In that situation, go with a more subtle darting bait, typified by the Lucky Craft Sammy. These very lifelike plugs have somewhat of a banana shape, making them ideal for "walking" in a zigzag pattern at a fairly fast pace.

BUZZING THROUGH AUTUMN

Rick Clunn was an early convert to buzzbaits. After a quarter of a century, he's still fine-tuning his techniques

WHEN OVERHEAD buzzbaits made their splashy entry into the world of bass fishing more than a quarter-century ago, Rick Clunn already had a couple of Bassmaster Classic appearances under his belt and was diligently laying the groundwork for his legendary status as a professional angler. The Lunker Lure soon became an essential lure in Clunn's arsenal, and it continues to put bass in his livewell today.

"A buzzbait is one of the most fun lures you can throw," says Clunn. "From a tournament standpoint, it produces the quality fish you desire. That's true of all topwater lures in general, but a buzzbait delivers a superior strike-to-catch ratio."

CONDITIONED BASS

In the early days of the buzzbait, Clunn scored well with it spring through fall, and even into the winter months. Bass also pounced on the buzzbait under a wide variety of weather and water conditions. Now that this lure has become one of the most widely fished baits on the planet, Clunn believes bass have become conditioned to it.

"Today, a buzzbait is mainly effective in late spring or early summer, and again in the fall," says Clunn. "In the fall, fishing pressure drops off, so bass don't see buzzbaits as often. And bass that spent the summer in deep water are moving into the shallows. They haven't seen a buzzbait for months and are more susceptible to it."

(Opposite page) DROPPING WATER temperatures draw shad into shallow water to feed on algae during autumn. As a result, the bass follow the bait, and a buzzbait is a productive lure for catching them.

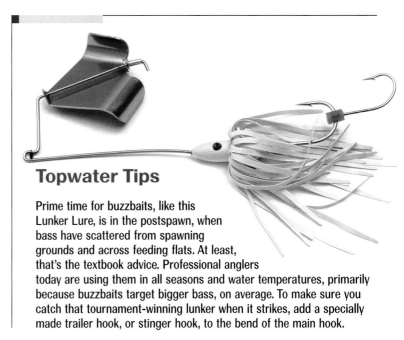

Topwater Tips

Prime time for buzzbaits, like this Lunker Lure, is in the postspawn, when bass have scattered from spawning grounds and across feeding flats. At least, that's the textbook advice. Professional anglers today are using them in all seasons and water temperatures, primarily because buzzbaits target bigger bass, on average. To make sure you catch that tournament-winning lunker when it strikes, add a specially made trailer hook, or stinger hook, to the bend of the main hook.

COLDWATER TOPWATERS

Whenever the water temperature is warmer than 50 degrees, a well-placed topwater plug might be the ticket

Z ELL ROWLAND, one of North America's most recognizable topwater anglers, competed in his first BASS tournament at the tender age of 13. The event took place at Table Rock Lake in November 1970, before a 16-year-old minimum age restriction was established on tournament competitors.

Having neither a boat nor tournament experience, Rowland tagged along with the partners he drew on each of the three tournament days. All were older, more experienced anglers who knew better than to fish surface baits in cold water, when bass are supposed to be deep and sluggish.

Rowland didn't let such preconceptions deter him from his favorite way to fish, which, of course, was with a topwater lure. Whenever his partners moved their boats within range of rock bluffs, Rowland cast a floating minnow tight to the bank and worked it with a twitch-and-pause action.

He stopped casting now and again to blow steamy breaths through his fists, but doggedly stayed with his topwater bait. Even snowstorms didn't dampen Rowland's enthusiasm, he says. You could chalk up his misguided strategy to youthful naiveté. Then again, his determination may have stemmed from the fact that, despite the frigid conditions, bass were coming up regularly and sucking in his floating minnow.

After two days of fishing, Rowland found himself in the top 20. He failed to catch enough bass on the final day to stay amongst the money winners, but was thrilled to do as well as he did against such celebrated anglers as Bill Dance, the eventual winner.

Another thing Rowland took away from the tournament was the knowledge that bass will take topwater baits in cold water. Even today, he fishes topwater baits in colder water than most of his competitors. This approach has paid off for him a number of times.

"I start fishing topwaters when the water reaches about 50 degrees in the spring," says Rowland, "and I stay with it until the water temperature drops below 50 degrees in the fall.

"When the water's cold, I throw a jerkbait (floating minnow). I'll twitch it and let it float. You have to fish slow because bass won't chase a fast moving lure then."

A Cordell 4-inch Red Fin ranks as Rowland's No. 1 surface bait when the water registers in the low 50s. The body of this 3/8-ounce lure is fatter

and thicker from top to bottom than other floating minnows. This results in more buoyancy, a slower, rolling action and a tendency to stay in place when twitched, all of which help tease lethargic, coldwater bass into action.

When bass prefer a more upbeat action, Rowland goes with a Smithwick Rogue, which features a slim body and a quick wobble. Whatever the bait, chrome with a black or blue back works well. He believes the red gills painted on the Red Fin greatly enhance this lure's bass appeal. Line size also plays an important role.

"I start with 20-pound-test monofilament in cold water," says Rowland. "A thick line is very buoyant and doesn't pull the minnow as deep when I twitch it."

Topwater Tips

One of the original minnow lures to be used as a jerkbait, the Smithwick Rattlin' Rogue has always been touted for its ability to catch coldwater bass. The combination of rattles and a very slim profile set it apart from most other twitch baits. Some pros enhanced the bait by drilling a hole in the belly and adding extra weight; this made the lure suspend motionless under water instead of rising to the surface, as most minnow baits do. Later, suspending jerkbait models were introduced by Smithwick and other manufacturers. Even without the weight, the tight wobble of a Rogue proves effective when wintertime bass are a bit more aggressive than normal.

If he doesn't get action with 20-pound line in 30 minutes or so, Rowland drops down to 14-pound test to let the lure dive deeper and work with more freedom. He emphasizes that subtle differences in action can be critical.

As for water color, clear is definitely better, especially in cold water. Rowland refuses to throw topwater lures in muddy water in any season. Lakes that feature clear water, steep banks and rocky bottoms yield the most consistent coldwater surface bite for Rowland.

"When the water temperature is 50 degrees on lakes like that," says Rowland, "I usually start out fishing bluff walls on the main lake where the water drops into 20 feet or more. Then I work my way back into a creek about three quarters of the way. I concentrate on steep banks, going from bluff walls to chunk rock banks and on to banks with smaller rocks as the creek starts to flatten toward the back. Usually, you're going to find fish on one of those three types of shorelines."

Any wood cover on steep rocky banks is likely to hold bass. Rowland favors fallen trees and works his topwater baits over upper branches that reach down into 8 to 10 feet of water.

"One thing anglers should remember," says Rowland, "is that not all bass move deep when a lake gets cold. Some will always be shallow, and they might be willing to hit a topwater bait. It usually isn't the most productive way to be fishing, but sometimes it'll surprise you."

Cold Front Tactics

If a cold front has moved in to disrupt your favorite topwater pattern, try lowering your expectations. Instead of throwing poppers and walking baits that skim the surface, cast a floating worm or surface minnow that will sink or dive just inches below your previous offering. Oftentimes, bass will still be in the mood to feed after a front, but will not be willing to make the extra effort to hit a bait floating on top. A couple of inches could prove to be the difference between an empty livewell and one brimming with post cold front bass.

One person who wouldn't be surprised is noted Ohio tournament angler George Polosky, who has been catching coldwater bass on top for more than 40 years. When Polosky was a 10-year-old bass fanatic, he didn't have multitudes of lures to choose from. One of his pet baits was a homemade, white pine popper designed by his older brother, Vic. The lure was about the size of a Pop-R, sported two treble hooks and was embellished with a rubber skirt.

"I would begin fishing that bait first thing in the spring," says Polosky. "There were times when I caught bass on the surface in 46 degree water. And those were shallow fish."

On one early spring outing, Polosky and his brother Vic rented a boat at LaDue Reservoir near Akron. They had to break ice to get under a bridge that led into the creek arm where they fished most of the day, without any luck.

On the way back that afternoon, they came upon a school of bass that had pushed small bluegill into a shallow pocket. In short order,

ADDING A FEATHER to a popper will enhance its strike appeal, and especially so if a fish has already made a pass at the lure.

they caught seven bass that weighed from 2 to 4 1/2 pounds on topwater baits. They had to break ice again on the way back to get under the bridge.

Today Polosky fishes his old homemade poppers on occasion, but relies mainly on the Rico, which he claims is superior to the many other poppers he has tested.

"The Rico is so buoyant that it rebounds when you pop it," says Polosky. "I like that quick reaction in a surface bait. I don't modify the bait at all, except to tie more feathers on the rear treble after the bass wear them off."

A 3/8-ounce buzzbait also plays heavily into Polosky's coldwater topwater fishing. He claims he always has a buzzbait tied on, regardless of the season.

"When I was growing up," says Polosky, "My brother, Vic, would tell me to fish a surface bait when everything else fails. I can't tell you how many times that has come through for me. On those days when I can't get a bite, I'll try a surface bait and get strikes. No matter what time of year it is, they will hit on top."

Whether he is casting a popper or a buzzbait, Polosky fishes with long spinning rods and bail-less spinning reels filled with 14-pound monofilament or Berkley's 30-pound-test Gorilla Braid. He grew up fishing spinning tackle and feels it helps him impart more lifelike topwater actions.

Many clear lakes have produced coldwater bass on surface baits for Polosky, but those supporting submergent aquatic vegetation, such as milfoil, yield more consistent results for him. The weeds exist beneath the surface, even in early spring.

"Normally," says Polosky, "I find bass in the backs of pockets both in the fall and spring. I catch a lot of fish in 5 to 6 feet of water, but they're often shallower than that."

In the fall, Polosky may catch bass on topwater baits throughout the day, but claims surface action sometimes dries up after midmorning. In the spring, midday to afternoon hours produce best for him. More important than time of day, believes Polosky, is the condition of the surface water.

"Anytime the water is calm," says Polosky, "you stand a good chance of catching bass on top. It doesn't matter what the barometric pressure is or whether it's sunny or overcast. Calm water is conducive to a topwater bite. I think bass just see the bait better."

Feathered Treble For Topwater Minnows

It's no secret that Zell Rowland dresses the rear trebles of his beloved Pop-Rs with chicken feathers, but few people know that he performs the same modification with floating minnows, especially when fishing on top in cold water.

"What I like about feathers," says Rowland, "is that you don't have to move the bait much to give them action. When you're twitching a surface bait slowly in cold water, the subtle movement of the feathers during a pause can make a big difference."

And when a bass swipes at a surface bait and misses, Rowland is convinced that the feathers encourage a second strike — provided you have the nerves to avoid setting the hook on the initial assault.

"Never set the hook until you feel the bass," says Rowland. "If it misses, let the bait sit. In most cases the bass is lying right under the lure, deciding what to do. When it sees the feathers quiver, he'll take another shot."

TOPWATERS ARE a savvy choice in fall because the fish are not accustomed to seeing them.

TECHNIQUES FOR TOPWATERS

The pros dig into their bag of tricks
to share their skills . . .

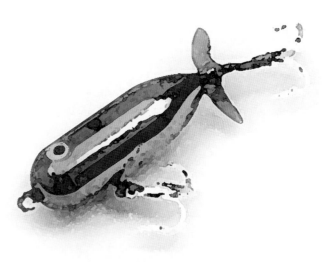

TOPWATERS ARE easily modified because they come in so many varieties. And making a subtle adjustment can make a huge difference in topwater success.

TOPWATER TRICKS OF THE PROS

Get an edge on the competition with these modified surface lures

ANY BASSMASTER worth his tacklebox knows that a topwater lure usually will work straight out of the package. Buy it, open it, tie it on and catch fish. But, sometimes a change, a single alteration of that lure, can mean the difference between a limit and an empty livewell.

The country's top pros regularly tweak their topwaters to increase their catch rates. Whether it's a minor adjustment to a buzzbait or a radical variation on a hard plastic lure, these expert anglers agree that a modification is often what separates the winners from the rest of the field.

Read on to learn how the pros tinker with their topwaters.

BENDING STEEL

One of Texas pro Zell Rowland's favorite tricks is to bend the blades on his Excalibur buzzbaits either in or out. By doing so, he can modify the speed at which he can retrieve a buzzbait without changing the size of his lure. Bend them in, and the blades dig deeper into the water, allowing Rowland to fish the lure slower. Bend the blades out, and he can pull it faster without disturbing the action that makes a buzzbait such a great lure.

"If I'm fishing in water 50 degrees or cooler, and I think a buzzbait is the right lure for the conditions, I'll cup the blades more than they are when they come out of the package," he says. "By doing that, I can fish a 1/2-ounce buzzbait real slow, and that's often the ticket for catching bass on top in cool water."

It's a simple task that doesn't require a single tool. Because most buzzbait blades are fairly soft, any angler can bend the blades with just a few fingers.

SWITCHING HOOKS

BASS world champion Mike Iaconelli invariably replaces the factory hooks on all his topwaters with high quality, needle-sharp treble hooks that are at least one size larger than the original hooks.

"The most important thing I do when I change hooks is put a larger treble on the back of the lure. By doing that, I'm weighing the tail of the lure down and forcing the nose of the bait to ride higher. That gives topwaters like a Mann's Chug-n-Spit a better splash, and it helps baits like a Zara Spook walk better," he says.

Iaconelli favors Gamakatsu treble hooks. On popping baits, he'll typically attach a No. 6 to the front eye and a No. 4 to the back eye. On larger baits, like Spooks, he'll put a No. 4 on the front

split ring and a No. 2 on the back one.

By adding those larger, sharper hooks, Iaconelli has seen his catch rate increase dramatically.

"If I'm throwing a topwater with a real high buoyancy and the nose still isn't riding like I want it to, I'll add some (Storm) SuspenStrips to the tail to weigh it down even more. Some baits tend to ride too high, so you don't get the right action out of them. Adding some weight will bring the lure down to the right level," he adds.

RUSTY RIVETS

To get more squeak out of an already noisy buzzbait, Virginia pro Rick Morris removes the factory installed aluminum rivet and replaces it with a steel rivet that he buys at a local hardware

Topwater Tips

Pros call it "the wiggle-diggle," and it's an easy trick to perform — if you have a modified Cordell Red Fin. Using a butane lighter, heat the plastic where the lip joins the throat of the lure. Bend the lip downward, until it's almost perpendicular to the body. It doesn't take much heat, and you should test-retrieve the lure in a swimming pool or along the lakeshore to make sure you don't bend the lip too far, or off-center. The 5-inch Red Fin is the preferred model. Properly modified, the lure should swim lazily from side to side, creating a wake as you reel it in slowly. You can wake a Red Fin without bending the lip, but the modification makes it so much easier. It's deadly on summertime bass.

Matching The Hatch

The pros take a variety of factors into consideration to squeeze every ounce of productivity out of surface lures.

Arkansas' George Cochran, who might be the most dedicated topwater fisherman on the tournament trail, borrows an old trout fisherman's trick by "matching the hatch" when selecting a surface bait. Whenever possible, Cochran determines the size of the prevalent baitfish in the area and matches it with a plug of similar length and color. For example, Cochran uses a Zara Spook to match the large summer shad on the Arkansas River, but switches to a 3-inch Baby Spook for the smaller shad that are so abundant in the winter on Alabama's Lake Martin.

Perhaps the most important aspect of productive topwater times — except for persistence — is paying close attention to the strikes these lures attract and learning from the behavior of each bass.

"When you catch that first bass, the fish is trying to tell you something," Larry Lazoen relates. "You have to be willing to listen. If you were hesitating your retrieve and got a strike, you need to slow down. If you were reeling it in to make another cast when the strike occurred, you should make a mental note that the bass was attracted to a quicker retrieve and that it wasn't tight to the structure or cover."

Successful topwater fishing may be 50 percent physical and 50 percent mental. These experts prove that with many anglers, the only limiting factor of these productive tools is the fisherman's mind set.

WHEN BASS ARE ACTIVE and chasing shad against the shoreline, savvy pros like their jerkbait to ride up on the surface to make commotion.

store. But first, he soaks the steel rivets in Clorox overnight.

"The bleach will rust the rivet, and by doing that, you get much more noise out of your baits," he says. "It's a great big bass tactic that has caught some real nice fish for me."

Morris simply straightens the L-bend that keeps the blade on the wire, removes the existing rivet and then replaces it with a rusted steel rivet. But before he uses it, he takes a file and roughens the edge of the blade that turns against the rivet. That adds even more noise to his Excalibur buzzbaits.

"I've found this tactic to be a great way to catch big bass in flooded pads in places like the Potomac River. It's my No. 1 warmweather pad bait," adds Morris. "You may go an hour or more without a bite, but I guarantee the fish

ADDING SPLIT RINGS to a topwater's hooks helps keep fish from throwing the lure when they jump, says Mike Iaconelli.

you do catch are going to be good ones. There is something about that squeaking noise that triggers big bass to bite."

HOOK SHIFT

When Texas pro Mark Pack ties on a Lake Fork Trophy Tackle Magic Shad, a soft jerkbait he manufactures and markets, he utilizes any of several hooking methods to control the action of his lure. By positioning the hook farther back or farther forward, he can determine whether his lure will stay close to the surface or sink beneath it.

"When bass are active and chasing shad against the bank or over open water, I want my jerkbait to ride up on the surface so it makes a lot of commotion. By rigging my hook so it rides toward the back of the lure, I can keep the bait up on top. It almost walks on the surface, like a Spook," he says.

To do that, Pack simply slides the hook about a half-inch into the nose of the bait before he pulls it through, turns it and brings the hook out the back of the lure. That shifts the weight toward the tail of the lure, which allows the nose to ride up. Each time Pack twitches his Magic Shad, it darts upward.

"It's a good tactic for fishing matted hydrilla, too. It doesn't get hung up in grass as much, and you can work it in the open pockets really well," he says.

Pack will also force his bait to stay under the water by inserting the hook only one-eighth inch or so into the nose. That shifts the weight to the front. Each time he twitches his rod tip, the lure tends to dip.

SPLIT RINGS

Another way New Jersey pro Mike Iaconelli modifies his topwaters is to add split rings to the hooks. In fact, it's a vital ingredient in his topwater arsenal, and he won't fish a surface bait without them. The reason is simple, he says: Split rings have nearly doubled the landing rate of bass he's hooked on topwater lures.

"Without a split ring, a bass has more leverage when it's pulling the hooks against the lure. With split rings, the hooks can rotate 360 degrees, and the bass can't get nearly as much leverage," he points

Tricks Of The Trade

Over the years, the pros have developed little tricks and tactics that, together, form a system of surface fishing that would seem to defy common beliefs. Through their collective experiences, these anglers have learned ways to stretch productive topwater times well past the traditional boundaries of hours, conditions and situations. And in the process, they have managed to snub conventional thinking about surface fishing in general.

"I don't know of another bait that has more misconceptions about it than topwater baits," claims Florida pro Steve Daniel. "Fishermen have developed certain ideas about these baits that they just won't let go of."

The myths commonly associated with topwater lures — those "early-and-late baits," for example — often destroy the very core of successful fishing that begins with having confidence in the tool being utilized.

"To be successful with topwater fishing, you have to have confidence in the lure you're throwing and the style of fishing you're doing," declares Sam Griffin, renowned Florida lure maker and the man Roland Martin has called "the world's premier topwater fisherman."

"If you don't have confidence in a lure, whether it be a topwater plug or whatever, you're not going to keep it tied on long enough to catch fish," Griffin says. "When you start swapping lures around, you might as well load your boat on the trailer, because you're not going to have a very good day. You can't keep going from one extreme to another — switching from a topwater plug to a worm and throwing it five times before going to a crankbait. You won't accomplish anything doing this. With topwater fishing, you need to put in enough time on the water — or your swimming pool — so that you understand the actions of the bait and feel confident fishing it."

More Topwater Tinkering

Few lures are modified more often than surface baits. Here are just a few of the pros' tricks for making them more productive under a variety of situations:

BUZZBAITS

■ **Hinging The Bait** — Oklahoma's O.T. Fears cuts the buzzbait wire in two, about 1/2-inch above the leadhead. He then attaches the two ends to a split ring by twisting the ends of the wire. "This allows the bait to ride lower in the water, which gives you a higher hooking percentage than you have with a standard buzzbait," Fear explains. "The split ring works like a hinge and allows the hook to swing free. It also prevents bass from using the bait's weight as leverage to throw the hooks."

ZARA SPOOK

■ **Tying Low** — Virginia pro Woo Daves files a tiny nick inside the lure's eye, enabling him to keep his knot at the bottom of the eye and ensure that he gets the proper action from the lure.
■ **Maltuning** — Guy Eaker tunes topwater lures like the Spook to run to one side or the other, similar to "maltuning" a crankbait. By slightly turning the line-tie eye of the bait, he can make it run well up under a boat dock or walk behind a tree.
■ **Free-Swinging Hooks** — Danny Correia of Massachusetts places a split ring between the hooks and the hook eyes. The result is a more free-swinging hook that eliminates leverage a bass might use to tear the hooks loose.

PROPELLER BAITS

■ **Prop Tuning** — George Cochran actually tunes the propellers on his surface lures so they make plenty of noise and leave a trail of bubbles similar to that of a buzzbait. To tune the props, Cochran screws out the prop shafts in opposite directions until each prop moves freely enough to spin with the slightest movement in the water.
■ **Drop A Prop** — Jay Yelas always removes the front prop of the Devil's Horse for a more subtle action. He also replaces stock trebles with premium extra-sharp hooks. Don't just cut off the hooks and add split rings, as some do — unscrew the hook hangers and swap out the hooks. The modified Devil's Horse works well on calm mornings.

POP-RS

■ **Shaving The Lip** — Yelas and other pros sometimes shave the entire lip of the Pop-R to make it sharper. This completely changes the sound it produces when quickly popped through the water. By sharpening the edge of the concave mouth, the Pop-R makes a light spitting sound instead of the heavy blurp commonly associated with chuggers. The pros theorize that this sound closely matches the noise made by frantic shad being chased across the surface of the water.
■ **Tail Dressings** — Ohio's Joe Thomas adds a flashy Mylar tail to chuggers like the Pop-R to give the bait a realistic flash similar to that of a live shad. Zell Rowland, the master of the Pop-R, ties a feather into the rear because it "pulses" better than the factory-issue bucktail when the lure is paused.

OTHER PLUGS

■ **Add Noise** — Lure designer Jim Gowing recommends adding rattles to otherwise silent topwaters by drilling a hole in the top of the bait, near the middle, and dropping in three or more BBs or other noisemakers. For a different sound, cut a pice of piano wire to about half the length of the bait, crimp a small split shot on one end of the wire and insert it into the lure. "You get an entirely different sound with the movement of the wire," he says.

A LOOP KNOT gives topwaters unrestricted movement, producing extra action.

out. "I also get a better initial hookup rate with split rings than without them."

Most lures come with eyelets that screw into the lure. The hooks are usually attached directly to those eyes. Iaconelli simply backs those out, cuts off the old hooks and inserts a split ring and a high quality Gamakatsu treble hook on the eyelet. On some lures, the hooks are attached to the lure with a small U-shaped piece of metal that is held to the lure with tiny screws. Iaconelli uses eyeglass screwdrivers to remove those.

BASS-ACKWARD

One of Tim Horton's favorite baits is a Heddon Baby Torpedo. Although he agrees that these lures are great straight out of the box, the Alabama pro immediately unscrews the front and back eyes and reverses them. In other words, he puts the line eye on the back of the lure, and the prop and rear hook on the front.

"Torpedoes come to a point in the back, and they are round at the front. By reversing that, I get the front, which now is the rear of the lure, to ride low in the water," he explains. "When I pull it, I get better spray in the front and more

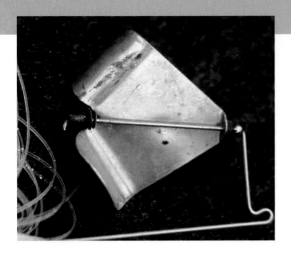

A RUSTY RIVET makes a buzzbait squeak and entices big bass to bite, claims Rick Morris, who replaces the factory's aluminum rivet with a steel version soaked in bleach.

spray from the prop in the back. An older gentleman showed me that years ago, and I've been using it ever since."

It's a trick Horton uses on both Tiny and Baby Torpedoes, and he simply matches his lure to the size of the baitfish. The only drawback is that on Torpedoes with eyes painted on them, the "prey" seems to be swimming backward.

"I don't think that matters too much, but if it does bother you, you can paint over them and paint new eyes in the front," he notes.

BIG BLADES

Missouri pro Chad Brauer sometimes finds himself in a situation in which a small, slow moving buzzbait is the right lure. But such baits can't be bought off the shelves, at least not buzzbaits that move at a snail's pace. So instead of switching to a new lure altogether, Brauer simply removes the factory blade from his 1/4-ounce Strike King Pro Buzz and replaces it with a blade from a 1/2-ounce model.

"The bigger blade really lets you slow down your retrieve. It's a great tactic in stained water, and I really like to use it in water that's between 55 and 65 degrees," he explains.

With a pair of needlenose pliers, Brauer straightens the L-bend that keeps the rivet and

blade on the wire, slides on the larger blade and bends the wire back in place. The 1/2-ounce blade works fine on the 1/4-ounce body, he adds, but if the gap between the blade and the wire is too small, you can simply bend it out a little.

BY ALLOWING his floating worm to sink a little as he moves his boat to the other side of a dock, Woo Daves can catch fish far up under the structures.

ONE OF THE MOST intense periods of topwater action occurs in the prespawn.

MIDDAY ACTION ON TOP

Bass might hit surface lures at any time of day. The angler's job is to be ready when conditions are right

IN BASS FISHING, the one rule of thumb that holds true all the time is this: There are no rules of thumb.

While some angling "rules" may apply most of the time, rest assured, there are always exceptions. And one area where the exceptions are large enough to accommodate several bass boats is topwater fishing.

For years, young anglers have been taught by their fathers and grandfathers that the dim light of morning and afternoon offers the prime opportunity for surface plugging. While the advice is well-intended, it falls wide of the mark as a bass fishing maxim.

Yes, reduced light and deep shadows do provide a helpful cover element for predators — and the surface activity may signal either the end or the beginning of an evening feeding spree. But bass can and do respond to surface lures at other times of the day. Unfortunately, the adage of "early and late" has stuck with us, and the hours between dawn and dusk have largely been ignored — for decades.

"We're raised as young bass fishermen with this mind-set," admits South Carolina Bassmaster touring pro Davy Hite. "But as you learn more about bass and their predator instincts, you realize that midday topwaters can be very productive."

The very same stories also have been passed down by generations of Western anglers, notes Arizona pro Greg Hines. "Traditionally, it has been an early-and-late

(Opposite page)
A TWITCH of a topwater bait can lure fish out from cover during midday.

Topwater Tips

While some experts consider the Baby Torpedo a "position bait" to be used with subtle movements, the lure can be surprisingly deadly over open, deep water. The technique works best in midsummer in clear lakes where spotted bass or smallmouth are prevalent. Bass often suspend away from cover, 20 or more feet under the surface, waiting for baitfish schools to happen by. Spotting suspended bass on your depthfinder makes it even more effective. Simply drift over open water where you suspect bass to be hanging out, make a long cast with the Baby Torpedo, then jerk it back to the boat in long, hard pulls. The slurping noise of the propeller draws bass from amazing depths. The Tiny version of the bait works just as well — the clear finish in either model seems to attract more strikes.

IN CHOPPY WATER, it may be necessary to switch to a heavier chugger, like this 3/4-ounce bait.

SUBTLE TOPWATER TRICKS

Whether you're fishing clear lakes of the West or the Northeast — or points in between — learn to work topwaters with finesse

I T'S HIGH NOON IN THE MOJAVE DESERT and the topwater bite is just about to turn on. Arizona bass pro Miles Etchart carefully searches through his tacklebox, selecting a chugger that best suits the choppy water. Although there are no signs to suggest the chugger will draw any interest, Etchart makes a long cast — up over the brush-filled cove.

The lure frantically scoots across the surface at a quickened pace — spitting water as it sashays back and forth. The chugger only gets about 20 feet before it disappears in a chaotic swirl. The tall, slightly built angler doesn't miss a single crank of his reel handle, battling the angry 3-pound desert bass to the boat.

Every fall, beginning in September and continuing well into November, the topwater bite on the Colorado River impoundments heats up. Count on it. However, says Etchart, anglers must make subtle adjustments in bait se...lection and presentation if they hope to score quality fish.

He has learned to match his topwater presentation with the surface conditions, water temperature and disposition of the bass.

The need to make fine adjustments in topwater presentation isn't unique to the West's desert impoundments; it's a recurring theme whenever bass are found in extremely clear water. Bass anglers in New England also find that small adjustments are important when chasing smallmouth.

Together, western pros Miles Etchart and Don Payne, and eastern stars Terry Baksay and Rick Lillegard explain how they make subtle changes in order to stay on top.

(Opposite page) **ANGLERS ARE required to make subtle adjustments in topwater presentations on ultraclear western impoundments.**

Topwater Tips

In Western reservoirs — indeed, in clear water anywhere in the country where shad are important forage — the spitting action of a small popping plug will bring lots of strikes. Not all poppers spit the same, however. The Iovino Splash-It is one of the best; try other brands and models to find one that works best in your waters. When bass are scattered across a feeding flat, or hiding within weedbeds or brushy areas, try a steady popping/spitting retrieve. Start with the rod tip held high and begin twitching and reeling simultaneously to make the bait spit continuously as you bring it in. Where bass (and perhaps stripers) are corralling big shad schools in open water, a more aggressive retrieve is in order. In that situation, reel quickly, pulling the bait a foot at a time to make it dart across the surface and throw long streams of water from its concave mouth.

SMALL TOPWATERS FOR FINICKY FISH

In calm water or other tough topwater situations, these tiny plugs can be the ticket to big bass

THE BULKY TOPWATER CHUGGER splashes across the surface of the lake, creating a disturbance capable of arousing slumbering bass anywhere in the vicinity. But it doesn't.

When this commotion fails to entice any bass, the angler concludes that the topwater bite is off and switches to a bottom-bouncing lure. This may seem like a logical decision to many Bassmasters, but in truth, they can still experience plenty of topwater thrills simply by downsizing their surface plugs.

"You can throw great big topwaters in windy conditions," says Cecil Kingsley, a veteran pro from Lawrence, Kan. "The windier it is, the bigger the topwater needed to hold the bait on the water and get the fish's attention. If the lake has slicked off calm though, bass are not going to bite that big lure like they will a small one."

Finesse topwater lures also produce well in clear water situations or on heavily fished lakes or rivers. The subtle action of these tiny lures triggers plenty of strikes, even from wary heavyweight bass.

On calm, bluebird days, Kingsley scales down to a Storm Baby Bug, which he throws on 8-pound-test line.

In stained water, he opts for a Baby Bug in firetiger or blue/chartreuse. If he's fishing a super-clear lake, such as Arkansas' Bull Shoals, he selects a clear Baby Bug and switches to 6-pound line, which allows him to make long-distance casts with the small lure.

He also favors the smallest member of the Rattlin' Chug Bug family when small baitfish are in the shallows.

(Opposite page)
WHEN THE WIND dies and the surface becomes calm, Kansas pro Cecil Kingsley relies on a Storm Baby Bug to catch bass on top.

Topwater Tips

It's important to use light line when fishing finesse-size topwater plugs like the Storm Baby Bug (shown here with a full-size Chug Bug). Since many situations calling for downsized topwaters involve clear water, 6- or 8-pound-test line will get more strikes than heavier line. What's more, lightweight plugs cast much farther and more accurately on light spinning tackle. Finally, heavy line will overpower the little plugs, robbing them of their subtle pops and darting movements. When fishing topwaters with light line, be sure to retie frequently, especially after catching a fish or two.

EX-STREAM EXCITEMENT: TOPWATERS FOR CREEK BASS

Topwater fishing for stream smallmouth and largemouth is not for the faint of heart

STREAM FISHING FOR BASS is at the opposite end of the angling spectrum when compared to the genteel sport of fly fishing for trout. Indeed, creek bassing is not about donning a pair of ultralight waders and casting a fly into a serene, trout-filled pool.

Those afflicted with creek fever willingly slog through miles of icy water, stumble their way around treacherous pools, risk breaking bones by slipping off slimy rocks and crunch across gravel

bars in 100 degree heat while kicking snakes out of their path. All, so they can reach the next pool where that big largemouth or smallmouth might be waiting.

There are plenty of ways to catch stream bass, but to a true creek junkie, nirvana is when a quality fish plasters a surface lure, cartwheels out of the water and crash-lands with all the subtlety of a Hawaiian shirt at a black tie dinner.

If you don't mind getting your feet wet and your hide scraped in your quest for bassing thrills, then read on. You'll meet two hard-core stream anglers who know topwater lures have powerful mojo when it comes to drawing big strikes in small waters.

BRONZEBACK BUZZWORDS

Avon, Ind., realtor George Verrusio is one of the cult's most adept stream smallmouth anglers. A master at coaxing big fish from alarmingly tight quarters, he's caught bronzebacks exceeding 4 pounds from Hoosier State streams you can practically jump across. The largest smallie of his wading career, a whopping 6-1, came from a Tennessee creek, and George isn't at all surprised he caught it on a topwater lure.

"I was wading a gravel-bottom creek in southwest Tennessee and catching smallmouth up to a pound and a half on grubs and finesse worms," Verrusio recalls. "Then I came to a deep hole with a sunken tree on the bottom. One of the branches angled up and broke the surface, creating a nice little backflow. This spot had 'buzzbait' written all over it."

A buzzbait, while a logical lure for largemouth in shallow cover, would hardly be the first choice of most stream smallmouth anglers. "All the more reason for me to try it," Verrusio says. "I figured the fish in this remote stream had never seen one."

He moved carefully within casting range, chunked the buzzer past the protruding limb and began a slow, noisy retrieve across the swift current. When the lure knocked against the branch and veered off crazily into the eddy, the biggest smallmouth of Verrusio's fishing career showed its true colors. "The bass blew totally out of the water, arched over and grabbed the buzzer," he recalls. "When it swam back down toward the tree, I told myself, even if the fish gets off, at least I got to see that amazing strike."

But the fish didn't get off. It turned and headed upstream, surfacing three more times in its attempts to shake the buzzer. Finally it tired; Verrusio lipped it, weighed it quickly on digital scales, and then released it back into the fast water.

"Needless to say, a topwater presentation is my first choice when stream conditions are right," he asserts.

And just what are those magic topwater conditions? Here are some cues Verrusio looks for in smallmouth streams:

• *60 to 70 degree water* — "I start throwing

Topwater Tips

The original Slug-Go, and especially Lunker City's Fin-S Fish, closely imitate minnows you're likely to find swimming in small rivers and streams. Try them in areas washed by current, such as large boulders and rock walls, where flow rates are highest. Cast upstream and across current, managing your line so that the lure drifts with the current and brushes against the obstacle. Twitch the rod tip occasionally to activate the soft jerkbait and watch your line for indications of a strike. In open areas of a stream, skip the Fin-S fish across the surface quickly to mimic a panicked minnow.

Finding Small Streams

Fishing creeks for smallmouth and largemouth bass is one of the least publicized forms of black bass angling. These small stream bass dwell in waters more often associated with trout than with bass.

In fact, they often live in tributaries of tributaries that flow into major rivers — small streams where 8 feet of water is deep, where the surrounding forest often forms a canopy over the water and where a host of avian and terrestrial predators combine to make these bass extremely wary.

Because stream fishing is so often ignored, finding a good one is not always easy and will require some work.

"You can't go into your local tackle shop and ask for information about the nearest place to go for creek bass," says Paul Calhoun, a professional photographer from Roanoke, Va., and a devoted stream angler. "With the emphasis on lake fishing today, chances are no one there will be able to help you.

"And the few guys out there who still creek fish usually aren't willing to help out. The bass fishing is so good and the fish are so unpressured that people in the know typically want to keep things a secret."

What Calhoun says anglers should do first is contact the DeLorme Mapping Co. (www.delorme.com; 800-561-5105). The firm publishes a number of state topo maps, and those maps include such features as backroads, stream access points, parks and forests. Another good resource is the Map Express (www.mapexp.com; 800-627-0039) in Boulder, Colo.

A good strategy is to locate a known quality smallmouth bass river on a map and then find tributaries to that river. The next step involves actually getting out and driving backroads to ascertain the size and potential of these tributaries.

Calhoun relates that some anglers like to fish near bridges, but he prefers to avoid these areas, because they receive too much fishing pressure. Instead, he talks to landowners well above or below bridges and gains access to a stream via private land.

The glory days for creek bass may have come and gone, and the fishing public might never again travel to these small waterways — as once was the habit when America was more rural and less populated. But the bass themselves still thrive in these streams and are well worth the effort to pursue.

topwater lures, including buzzbaits, about three or four weeks before the spawn, and stay with them until the water rises above 70 degrees. The smallmouth topwater bite usually slacks off in midsummer, and then picks back up again in the fall."

• *When the grub/worm bite turns off* — "I catch the majority of my stream smallies on lead-head grubs and finesse worms rigged on Slider heads, but if I'm not getting bit on these standbys, I'll often get a good response to a topwater lure. Smallmouth are moody fish, and sometimes they'll smack something on the surface out of sheer orneriness."

• *Where big fish are a possibility* — "Of course, 'big' is a relative term — in many smallmouth streams, a 2-pounder is a rarity. But creeks with good habitat that don't get much pressure can hold surprisingly large smallies. While wading streams in the Southeast, I've seen fish I'm certain were over 7 pounds. If you're after a trophy fish, run a topwater lure around some prime creek structure and hang on. At times, big smallmouth are more catchable with a surface presentation than with any other approach."

• *Major hatches* — "Stream smallies eat a lot of insects, and sometimes a major bug hatch can trigger a tremendous topwater bite. The best week of creek topwater fishing I ever experienced was during a cicada hatch. These big bugs were dropping out of shoreline trees, and smallies were nailing 'em as they floated on top. Any surface bait you threw at them would get eaten immediately."

GEARING UP FOR SMALLIES

Verrusio recommends the following topwater lures for creek smallies:

• *Buzzbaits* — "My top surface pick for big fish. Stream smallies are like muskies — sometimes you have to cast to them repeatedly before they'll bite. I may run a buzzer past a likely-looking log or rock 20 times from different angles. Always use a stinger hook with a buzzbait."

• *Floater/diver minnows* — "Rapala and A.C. Shiner minnows are hard to beat in clear creeks. I rig mine with a split ring for more fluid action. Twitching the minnow on top around cover works, but also try slow swimming it over the surface so it throws a wake, the way striper fishermen retrieve a Red Fin. I normally recommend natural colors in creeks, but I've caught some dandy smallmouth on a white A.C. Shiner with a hot-orange belly. Go figure."

• *Poppers* — "Ideal for pulling a big fish out of cover. Cast a Pop-R next to a submerged rock or logjam and pop it repeatedly — this is the topwater equivalent to shaking a worm."

• *Soft jerkbaits* — "Skipping a Slug-Go or Fin-S Fish across the surface like a panicked shad can trigger a violent strike. Use the lure's worm hook as a hanger for a small free-swinging treble hook; this stinger will stick fish that only take a swipe at the lure."

• *Stickbaits* — "Heddon's Zara Puppy is a good size for creek smallies. Walk it over submerged cover in quiet pools where current is diminished."

• *Crawlers* — "The classic Jitterbug and Crazy Crawler are awesome stream lures in low light situations, and when the water is off-color after a rainstorm. Use a slow, steady retrieve."

• *Prop baits* — "Lures like the Tiny Torpedo are good topwater choices on rainy or windy days, but don't overfish 'em."

POPPERS LIKE these Bug-I lures rate high for big stream bass. For best results, vary the number and intensity of pops until you find what triggers bass to strike.

A GOOD LURE choice when stream bass are busting insects on the surface is Heddon's Crazy Crawler.

LARGEMOUTH LOGIC

Nashville songwriter Jeff Pearson approaches creek fishing with all the focus and intensity of a tournament angler. As he puts it, "There are stream anglers who are there mainly to enjoy the birds and wildflowers, but I'm not one of them. The only reason I get my feet wet is to catch bass." And he does this quite well, thank you — Pearson's biggest creek largemouth weighed nearly 7 pounds.

Topwater lures play a huge role in Pearson's fishing.

"I use surface baits to monitor the mood of the fish," he notes. "The first lure I have tied on when I step into the creek in

USE SURFACE BAITS
to monitor the mood
of the fish.

the morning is a topwater plug. Often, it'll get hit within the first few minutes by a small bass or even a bluegill; this tells me there's some feeding activity going on and helps me fine-tune my presentation to attract a bigger bass.

"If it's totally ignored, I'll switch to a subsurface lure, like a spinnerbait or small crankbait."

Pearson has had surprisingly good results on topwaters in early spring, when the water is frigid.

"Most fishermen think the water is way too cold for a surface presentation in late February or March, but a creek is a different environment than a lake. Stream largemouth survive by snatching a meal when and where they can, and they won't often hesitate to take it off the surface, even in 45 degree water."

Pearson's favorite topwater style for stream largemouth is the popper. He's had tremendous success on Japanese spitting lures, such as the Michael Bait and Splash-It, but admits most waders may be reluctant to chunk these premium-priced baits in snaggy streams.

"The Rebel Pop-R is a less expensive alternative; try the Ultra-Lite model in natural colors," he suggests.

Floating minnows also rate high with Pearson. "Use a minnow big enough to cast easily, but no bigger than the prevalent forage in the creek," he advises. "Creek largemouth will often take a Rapala entirely differently than they'll hit a Pop-R. They'll swim up and suck it

IF YOU FIND an isolated logjam serving as a current break, twitch a hard minnow near the structure and hang on.

More Creek Bass Tips

Want more surface strikes in streams? Try these inside tips from expert creek anglers George Verrusio and Jeff Pearson:

■ Don't let a lack of surface activity deter you from trying a topwater presentation. The compact environment of a stream makes these lures especially deadly on big bass, even when they're not actively feeding.

■ In clear creeks, a slow surface retrieve often draws more lookers than strikers. Try working a minnow lure or soft jerkbait quickly across the surface for an aggressive strike.

■ If bass boil on your surface lure but won't take it, try a fallback lure, such as a finesse worm, grub or slow sinking Slug-Go, in the same spot.

■ The wading angler doesn't have the luxury of carrying multiple rods, so the stick he chooses must be able to handle all types of lures. Pearson likes a 6-foot medium action spinning rod; Verrusio prefers a 6 1/2-foot medium-heavy spin stick.

■ Overhand casting can mean constant hang-ups when targeting shoreline cover with treble-hooked topwaters. In hard-to-reach spots, work close to your target with short underhand pitches. Camo waders and clothing will help conceal your presence in clear water.

■ Experiment with retrieve direction when using different topwater styles. Pearson prefers to retrieve minnow lures and poppers with the current; Verrusio has had good results retrieving buzzbaits against the current.

■ Remember that catch-and-release of quality bass is essential to future stream productivity.

in gently. Before setting the hook, you've got to make yourself hesitate a second until the bass takes it completely under."

Pearson knows largemouth stick to slow moving or slack water in streams; he targets his casts tight to current-breaking objects, like lay-down logs, weedbeds and rocks.

"A good rule of thumb when you're after a lunker largemouth in a creek is to cast to spots where there's a high risk of getting hung up," he notes. "Deep, dark eddies; snaggy holes with a slow flow; under-cut banks with low-hanging branches; logjams — that's where big creek bass hang out. Some of these spots may have a window of only a few inches where you can present the lure without getting hung up. Short, accurate presentations are a must."

Pearson varies his topwater retrieve constantly until he determines what the bass want. "The biggest mistake I see most creek fishermen make with surface lures is using the same retrieve over and over," he says. "This may work on small bass, but you've got to mix it up for a big fish. Sometimes lunker largemouth want a real inactive presentation. "I've caught some real wall-hangers by twitching or popping the lure once or twice, then letting it sit dead in the water for almost a minute.

"Then there are days when it seems you can't retrieve it fast enough — it's a rush seeing a big bass shoot out from a sunken tree to grab a fast moving Rapala."

THE CLASSIC JITTERBUG is a productive stream lure in low light conditions.

SMALLMOUTH ON THE SURFACE

Catching the gamest bass
in the lake on top . . .

SMALLMOUTH ON TOP

To these pros and guides, heaven on earth occurs whenever smallmouth take a shine to surface baits

AS A GUIDE ON PICKWICK, Wilson and Wheeler lakes, Tim Horton was one lucky guy. Now a well-known and successful pro, Horton honed his angling talents on this threesome of Tennessee River impoundments known for their world class smallmouth fishing. And the best part of his former job was the times when the smallmouth were on top.

"I've been fortunate enough to fish all over the country, and I can tell you there's nothing like catching smallmouth on top," Horton says. "Not only is it a great way to catch fish, but it's the most exciting way, too.

Topwater Tips

Smallmouth absolutely love stickbaits like the Zara Spook, but there are times when a more compact darting bait, such as the Excalibur Spit'n Image (shown here), is even better. The lure looks so much like a live shad that fishermen have even reported seeing schools of shad minnows following the bait. You can "walk the dog" with the Spit'n Image, just like the zigzag pattern of a Spook. But in moving water and when trying to call smallmouth from greater distances, fish the bait more aggressively, with more slack in the line. A sharp jerk causes the bait to roll on one side, and the next pull makes it spit water loudly, like a school of fish in a feeding frenzy.

"I guess the blowups are probably the most exciting part of it. Of course, when you hook them and they're jumping around, and you've got other smallmouth trying to take the bait away from them — that's incredibly exciting. But it can be just as exciting when they come out of the water and crash down on the bait."

"There's nothing like seeing those big smallmouth charge up from below and hammer a topwater bait," adds Jim Morton, an Oklahoma pro and former BASS winner. "There's not a more enjoyable way to catch them. And in some cases, it is the *best* way to catch them."

It might surprise some bass enthusiasts to learn that there is prime topwater smallmouth exhilaration to be had throughout much of the year. With the proper approach, surface action on smallies can stretch from the spring spawn through the fall. And fall might just be the best time of all for calling these bronze-colored torpedoes to the surface.

"From spring through fall on the Great Lakes, I fish with people using a jerkbait or spinnerbait," Ohio pro Joe Thomas relates. "They might be outcatching me 3-to-1, but I'll keep throwing my Pop-R or Spook because I know the fish are going to be bigger, and the strike is going to be awesome."

TIM HORTON: SUMMER TILL FALL

During his guiding days on the Tennessee

River, the summer and fall months were a particular favorite for Horton's customers. That's because of his ability to follow the seasonal migrations of Pickwick's big smallmouth to ensure that the prime time topwater excitement lasted for months.

"Good topwater fishing can last from late May through most of November on lakes like Pickwick," Horton says. "In the summer, we usually find the fish to be at the head of an upriver point, usually where it makes the sharpest break and forms an eddy. They wait there in 4 and 5 feet of water and ambush shad. The neat thing about it is, when the current is running, you can watch it on a calm day and see the shad rippling the top of the water in big schools. And after three or four

minutes, they come drifting down these ridges — and shad 'school' is in session for these big smallmouth.

"But if I had to pick the absolute best topwater month, it would be October. October is a 10 when it comes to topwater smallmouth. It's good from mid-September through early November, as the water continues to cool."

When the region begins experiencing 50 degree nights in September, Horton follows the shad as they start migrating into the shallow backs of creeks, where the smallies begin gorging themselves in preparation for winter. This is a situation in which the surface action can last throughout an entire day — producing as many as 50 fish per day in the 3- to 6-pound range.

TIM HORTON PICKS
October as the prime month for catching smallmouth on top-waters.

seems like when they can see the flash or silhouette of that bait against the sun, you can really catch them. But the key is calm, flat water. I don't care what the sky conditions are — if you have calm, flat water, they will just absolutely come up and crush a topwater bait."

When searching for smallmouth that might be susceptible to a surface offering, Thomas targets scattered chunk rock surrounded by vegetation in 7 to 11 feet of water. This is the kind of place where a bronzeback won't hesitate to charge to the surface to assault a lure.

Thomas' all-time favorite topwater for smallmouth is a Rico chugger (tied to 14-pound-test green Stren monofilament) that he retrieves with a rhythmic, snapping cadence. Working the bait too slowly usually leads to short-striking bass that seem to quickly lose interest in the bait, he says. And in his opinion, it is almost impossible to retrieve the Rico too rapidly.

"I also throw a Spook a lot, which will usually catch the larger fish," Thomas adds. "But with the Spook, smallmouth end up playing volleyball with it a lot, without getting the hooks in their mouths."

JIM MORTON: BLUFF BANK BRONZEBACKS

Morton is a different breed of cat in his part of the country. He is one of the few bass enthusiasts in southeastern Oklahoma who actually targets smallmouth in the emerging fisheries found in lakes like Texoma and Murray.

The clear water of late spring through summer brings the most productive time for luring trophy-class smallmouth to the surface. Morton enjoys some tremendous topwater action on gold- or chrome-colored chuggers, like the Storm Rattlin' Chug Bug, through late August, when the water is as hot as it will get.

Morton finds his best concentrations of summer smallmouth around bluff banks with huge boulders that sit in 15 to 40 feet of water. Using 10- or 12-pound line, he parallels the rocks instead of casting to them from deeper water.

"I work the rocky bluffs just like you would a wall of riprap," Morton says. "In the summer, it seems like the faster the retrieve, the better those big smallmouth like it. These fish will really gang up in the summer. It's nothing to catch three or four off the same big boulder."

RICK LILLEGARD: THE SPOOK FAN

Like a legion of bass anglers living in smallmouth country, BASS pro and New England guide Rick Lillegard is a huge fan of the Zara Spook. Although he employs four basic types of surface plugs in his home region from postspawn through fall, Lillegard is a devotee of the original Spook and the fairly new Super Spook Junior.

THE SPIT'N IMAGE is one of Tim Horton's most productive surface baits for smallmouth.

Topwater Retrieves

Whether you're after smallmouth or largemouth, surface plugs are used in one of two quite different applications: broad areas, such as a large patch of vegetation, a flat covered with standing timber, a sunken island or a riprap bank; and specific, confined spots usually featuring one dominant cover object. Examples of the latter include a laydown log, stump, brushpile, bridge piling or small weed patch.

The situation determines the retrieve, say two veteran BASS pros from Arkansas, George Cochran and Ricky Green.

"In a confined area," says Green, "you're fairly sure that if a bass is present, it's holding close to these cover objects, so you fish slower and use baits with a subtler approach."

Cochran adds, "If I could pass on just one tip about fishing topwaters, this would be it: Don't get in too big a hurry. Most people don't wait long enough before starting their retrieve. When I'm fishing a floating lure, especially near an object, I'll force myself to let my bait rest at least 30 seconds after it hits the water.

"This is because a bass instinctively wants to kill something that's crippled, even if it doesn't want to eat it. So if you cast a bait into a spot and leave it there and let that fish have plenty time to watch it and get irritated by it, so many times it'll nail the bait when it makes that first little twitch or jerk."

"If I'm fishing an area as opposed to a spot or object, I won't wait so long before I start my retrieve, and I'll probably work the bait faster," Green clarifies. "For instance, if I'm fishing a stump or log with a prop bait, I'll do so ever so slowly. But if I'm pulling a Pop-R along the edge of a grassline, I'll start popping it as soon as it hits, and I'll keep it coming right along."

Both anglers stress the need to try different baits and retrieves to see which the fish prefer on any given day. Green says, "Sometimes they'll want a walking bait; other days a popper. So once you decide whether you're fishing specific spots or broad areas, then you just have to experiment within that bait group to see what's working the best. Don't try to tell the fish what to hit — let them tell you."

"My No. 1 choice for smallmouth in our natural lakes is the Spook in a gold-chrome color for partially sunny days and a black-shore-minnow-colored Spook for bright days," he says. "I have had good success throwing topwaters right in the middle of the day in bright sunshine.

"There is really no bad time to throw a topwater for smallmouth."

Lillegard's idea of a perfect Spook day would feature calm waters and overcast skies with a slight drizzle. But he has enjoyed some memorable smallmouth days in less-than-ideal conditions with the venerable cigar-shaped stickbait.

"The key to catching the biggest smallmouth on top is making real long, high casts and making the biggest splash possible when it hits the water," he adds. "Then I let it sit there for as long as I can stand it. We've all heard the old adage about letting the circle disappear. Well, I do it a lot longer than that sometimes. I truly believe the splash gets the attention of these fish. A lot of times, fish in the 4-pound range will just take it sitting still off the surface if you will leave it sitting there 30 to 45 seconds."

For short-striking smallmouth, Lillegard switches to the smaller Spook Junior, which is easier for the supercharged bass to inhale.

THE ERRATIC side-to-side movement of a Zara Spook is irresistible to smallmouth.

THE WATER churning action of a buzzbait stands out in white-water.

BUZZBAITS FOR WHITE-WATER BRONZEBACKS

Surface buzzers are hot lures for trophies on West Virginia's top smallmouth rivers

ENTION THE BUZZBAIT that splashes about on the water surface like a frantically swimming bird, frog or fish, and many bass anglers will say, "It's a great lure for fishing those open spaces between lily pads or for early morning or late evening casting, when there's no wind to push up wavelets. Works great on a glass-smooth stream, pond or lake."

They are not, of course, wrong. But too few of those anglers, while striving to attract lunker smallmouth, would select the buzzbait to cast into the turbulent whitewater of a fast moving moun-

tain river. If not, they could be missing the pleasure of almost continuous bass fishing action and also, quite often, the excitement of bringing a trophy fish to boat.

Bass anglers who have fished West Virginia's New and Greenbrier rivers with veteran fishing guides have learned the truth of this statement. From about the first of June through September, some guides use little else but buzzbaits on these rivers, rarely switching to other lures during a 14 hour day.

Earlier in the year, before the water temperature

BUZZBAITS CAN ALSO be fished in areas adjacent to rushing water when the fish frequent feeder creeks to hunt prey.

gets above 70 degrees, fishermen do well with a jig-and-pig or with shallow running spinners.

"But after the first of June," says one guide, "we begin to hammer them with buzzbaits."

They often use and recommend buzzbaits that kick up a lot of water with their spinning blades. Like many other bass anglers of long experience, the river rats frequently modify any commercial product. If, for instance, the spinning blades revolve about a wire too near the skirted hook, they shorten the wire to place the blades farther forward. And they usually add a large, white grub behind the skirt.

For steady action, cast buzzbaits into whitewater and adjacent swift water that cuts around boulders and under overhanging trees. Not only do buzzbaits catch a lot of smallmouth, they are also consistent producers of lunkers. You don't catch as many smallmouth with buzzbaits as with some other lures, but they bring in the trophy fish.

This does not mean that you are going to sit for hours watching your buzzbait flutter while nothing happens. Far from it. On an average day in a single hour, you are going to get many strikes and several small- to medium-size smallmouth while waiting for that big one to get hungry or mad at that noisy intruder in its territory.

If you put a large grub on the skirt-covered hook of your buzzbait, you are going to get many short strikes at the grub's waggling tail. You won't hook the fish — but that is part of the grub's function. On the New River, if you had to remove the hook from every juvenile smallmouth that bothered your buzzbait, you would soon weary of a time-consuming activity.

The New and Greenbrier rivers rank high as smallmouth streams and are considered by many as No. 1 and No. 2, respectively, in the Mountain State.

The Greenbrier, a New River tributary, is a much smaller stream than the latter, but shares nearly all of the New's characteristics of interest to sportfishermen. It does not, like the New, have Class VI white-

water. Because of the great number of whitewater rafters finding thrills in the lower New River, not many anglers choose to chase smallmouth in this often-dangerous and crowded section.

Most whitewater fishing in the New River is done from the great Bluestone Dam at Hinton to a section of the river near Prince. The most heavily fished part of the river may be from the mouth of the Greenbrier, just below Bluestone Dam, to Brooks Falls, which is the name of a town and a waterfall, a distance of about 10 miles. A little farther downstream is Sandstone Falls, a landmark and favored fishing spot. You will not, unless you're a daredevil rafter or kayaker, attempt to ride your craft over Sandstone Falls.

But the New River, like the Greenbrier, is basically, under normal conditions, a shallow stream. When the river is clear (which it usually is) you may use your polarized glasses to see the bottom everywhere except for some deep pools or where boiling water obscures vision. This means you may often see the smallmouth striking your bait, or about to do so.

Topwater Tips

Who knows what a buzzbait resembles to a smallmouth bass living in whitewater sections of rivers? Fleeing baitfish? A terrestrial creature that has fallen into the water? A duckling that couldn't stay out of the current? Whatever the answer, smallmouth won't often pass up a fast-moving, noisy buzzer churning through the foam. To keep the bait riding high in the current, add a plastic grub for a trailer. The extra length it adds to the lure doesn't seem to bother the fish, and it makes it much easier to keep the buzzer on the surface. Don't overlook buzzbaits in calmer sections of rivers, either. They'll draw savage strikes in riffles as well as they will in eddies.

THE DENSITY OF SOFT STICKBAITS
enables anglers to cast them far and
cover lots of water.

SOFT STICK-WORMS FOR SMALLMOUTH

These cigar-shaped soft jerkbaits are the rage among smallmouth anglers in the know

WHEN SOFT PLASTIC jerkbaits hit the tackle shop shelves over a decade ago, few anglers realized how revolutionary they would be. Not only were they the most exciting new lure to hit the market in a long time, they were perhaps the most effective at catching bass under the right conditions.

Just when anglers thought that there was nothing left to invent, a new lure has been introduced, and like Slug Gos, which spawned a frenzy among lure manufacturers as well as anglers, this one is the beginning of a new soft plastic craze. Meet the Yamamoto Senko, the Hawg Caller Teezo and the Cabin Creek Salty Sinkin' Worm — the hottest lures to hit the smallmouth world in a long time.

If you listen to fans of these soft stickworms, you'd think there was no wrong way to fish these lures. Impale them on a hook, chuck them out and wait for a bite. If that sounds a bit too simple, guess again. That's about all there is to it.

Senkos, Salty Sinkin' Worms and Teezos all have a similar cigar shape with a tapered blunt end and a slightly more pointed end. Although most anglers start by rigging them with the hook through the blunt end, Alabama pro Randy Howell will use the other end when the fatter side gets torn up.

"I haven't seen much of a difference in my catch rates when I use either end. That's a great way to get more mileage out of these lures," he says. "I don't know what it is about these lures the fish like so much, but they work better than many other types of tried-and-true smallmouth lures."

Why are these lures so effective? Those who use them say it has more to do with the salt content than the shape of the lure. Although the profile looks so ordinary, so lifeless, it's the sink rate, combined with a shimmying wiggle, that entices smallmouth to eat this lure with reckless abandon.

Drop one in the water next to your boat and you'll see for yourself. They fall faster than most other soft plastic lures, and they have a slight, tantalizing wiggle as they sink. They look like nothing in nature, but smallmouth don't care. They grab them and hold on, thanks to the high salt content, experts agree. They also credit the soft texture. Whatever the reason, soft stickbaits are hot smallmouth lures.

RIGGING UP

There are indeed a variety of ways to fish these featureless baits, but as Howell says, they are so new, "we haven't figured out all the uses for them yet." Most anglers use soft sticks with either of two quick and easy rigging methods: Texas rigged or wacky style. Most anglers fish them without any sort of weight, although Howell and Stan Scott, a BASS angler from Richland, Wash., will vary their hooks to control sink rates. Heavy-gauge hooks pull the bait down a little more quickly; fine-wire hooks allow the baits to sink somewhat slower.

What they use depends on a few variables, but as Howell says, sometimes rigging methods don't seem to matter. He's caught smallmouth both ways during a single day.

Topwater Tips

Soft stickworms, like this Berkley Gulp Sinking Minnow, are dynamite on big smallmouth throughout the year, especially in clear to slightly stained water. Prime times are spring and fall, when smallies are most likely to be shallow. In those situations, Texas rig the bait with 4/0 wide gap hooks, or wacky rig them (with a 3/0 hook through the middle). After casting, let the bait sink for several seconds as you pay close attention to your line. Set the hook if you see the line twitch — otherwise, the fish is likely to swallow the bait. If the lure doesn't get bit on the first descent, twitch it two or three times and let it settle again. The wobbling sinking motion seems to be an irresistible trigger for smallmouth to strike.

Budget Soft Sticks

It's no secret that Senkos are expensive, but just because a lure is a little torn up doesn't mean it's destined for the dump. They can be salvaged. And they can be altered to last a little longer during their initial use.

Potomac and Shenandoah River guide Tim Freese wraps a small piece of electrical tape around the middle of his Senkos and runs his hook through the tape. That keeps the hook from tearing through the lure on a hook set or from the thrashing of a smallmouth — a real problem with Senkos.

Freese also suggests melting the plastic back together with any of the products meant for such a job. He uses a battery-powered Worm Miser, similar to a wood-burning tool. The high salt content makes the task of melting the lures back together a little tougher, but it can be done, at least for a few more fish.

SMALLMOUTH CAN'T resist the subtle action of a soft stickbait.

"I was fishing a tournament on Lake St. Clair right after Hawg Caller sent me a bunch of these Teezos. A couple of my friends on the tournament trail raided my boat and took several bags of my favorite color," he recalls.

Halfway through the tournament, Howell, who had been Texas rigging these lures (without a weight), ran out. That is, he ran out of new lures that weren't torn up on both ends. Fortunately, he had enough foresight to leave the used Teezos in the bottom of his boat, offering a rag-tag assortment of soft sticks.

"I just started wacky rigging the lures that were too torn up on the ends. That worked just as well," says Howell.

Scott typically rigs his wacky style, running a 1/0 Owner Mosquito hook through the egg sack, an ideal presentation for heavily pressured smallmouth. He claimed second place in a Western Invitational held on the Columbia River in a high-pressured area by doing exactly that.

"I was fishing a well-known community hole that produces a lot of big smallmouth. In fact, there have been quite a few tournaments won from that spot. There were eight or 10 boats working this one small area, but just about everybody else was throwing tubes or drop shot rigs and not catching many fish. I caught a 20-pound bag of smallmouth the first day, all on 5-inch Senkos," he recalls.

Howell utilizes both rigging styles as well, preferring the wacky-rigged Teezo when the fish are less active and less eager to chase a bait. He'll Texas rig it on a 4/0 Daiichi Bleeding Bait wide gap hook when the bass are more active, and he'll work it a little faster.

FISHING METHODS

Both experts agree that these lures shine when they do nothing, and prefer to dead-stick these baits and let the lures speak for themselves. Again, they have a subtle shimmy as they sink, which seems to be all the action a smallmouth needs to see.

"I just throw them out and let them sink," says Howell. "They cast a mile, which is ideal in heavily pressured water or when the water is real clear. That's pretty typical of most smallmouth lakes, anyway. The fish will come from a long way to eat one of these baits."

Scott agrees. He typically throws his lure out and lets it free-fall toward the bottom, keeping a close watch on his line as the bait sinks. He prefers to fish these lures with Power Pro braided line tipped with a fluorocarbon leader because the braided line floats, acting like a bobber of sorts.

THROW SOFT JERKBAITS when the water climbs into the high 50s.

Weighted Jerkbait Techniques

When smallmouth bass aren't overly aggressive, guides Lou Giusto of the Shenandoah River and Vermont's Jim Sweeney weight their soft jerkbaits and slow their retrieves. The thin shape of these lures still looks tantalizing enough to attract a bass, and the texture feels realistic to a fish. Fish hold on to these lures much longer than they hang on to hard baits.

Sweeney, who likes to sight fish for bedded smallmouth on Vermont's clear lakes, knows that spawning fish sometimes aren't in a mood to chase a lure. In these situations, he inserts a nail into the bait for weight and lets it settle over a bed. Often, the weight will help keep the bait in a slow, straight free fall, right into the bed.

After the spawn, bass retreat to deeper water, and the Vermont guide slowly pulls a weighted Floozie over water as deep as 20 feet.

"The bass suspend, and in this clear water, they will come up a good ways to hit a bait," he says.

Giusto has discovered that hard-to-catch smallmouth will often pick up a Fluke that is either sitting idle or rolling along the bottom.

"I weight mine with a 1/32-ounce slip sinker and just let it rest on the bottom in pockets behind boulders and in slower moving water," he says.

"I can also cast much farther with Power Pro line and I can detect real soft bites, which are pretty common with these baits. The fish often just swim up and suck it in. They don't always slam it like they do other lures," he says.

The key, both experts agree, is to fish these lures on a fairly tight line, keeping an eye out for subtle twitches or other movement in your monofilament. You can't keep it too tight, warns Scott, because that will ruin the free-falling action of the lure.

Howell will twitch his lure to bring it back up toward the surface and then let it fall again as he works it back to the boat. Scott utilizes a similar twitching method, but he says the vast majority of strikes come on the fall, so it's important to get the lure up away from the bottom before allowing it to sink again.

"I won't fish it on windy days because I just can't detect strikes. Other than that, there aren't many limiting factors to when I'll use a Senko," says Scott.

ADVANCED STICKING

Gary Yamamoto's Senkos originally came in 4-inch and 5-inch versions, but a demand for finesse-type baits coaxed him to develop a 3-inch stick. Although they are far less popular among smallmouth anglers, 3-inch soft sticks have a dedicated following.

Deep bass are a little tougher to reach, but Howell will rig a Teezo on a Carolina rig, and he's heard of reservoir smallmouth anglers rigging them on an open-hook jighead and using them in place of finesse worms. Others add a nail weight to the tail of the lure to hasten the sink rate and to give the lure a different look as it falls.

FISH SOFT jerkbaits around eddies, fast riffles, shallow flats and other areas that might hold smallmouth in warming water.

INDEX